GOSPEL
THE BOOK OF
MATTHEW

A NEW TRANSLATION WITH COMMENTARY—
JESUS SPIRITUALITY FOR EVERYONE

GOSPEL
THE BOOK OF
MATTHEW

THOMAS
MOORE

Walking Together, Finding the Way®
SKYLIGHT PATHS®
PUBLISHING
Nashville, Tennessee

Gospel—The Book of Matthew:
A New Translation with Commentary—Jesus Spirituality for Everyone

© 2016 by Thomas Moore

Library of Congress Cataloging-in-Publication Data
Names: Moore, Thomas, 1940– translator, writer of added commentary.
Title: The Book of Matthew : new translation with commentary—Jesus spirituality for everyone / Thomas Moore.
Other titles: Bible. Matthew. English. Moore. 2016.
Description: Quality paperback edition. I Woodstock, VT : SkyLight Paths Publishing, [2016] I Series: Gospel I Includes bibliographical references.
Identifiers: LCCN 2016005671I ISBN 9781594736209 (hardcover) I ISBN 781594736254 (ebook) I ISBN 9781683363453 (paperback)
Subjects: LCSH: Bible. Matthew—Commentaries.
Classification: LCC BS2573 2016 I DDC 226.2/05209—dc23 LC record available at http://lccn.loc.gov/2016005671

Manufactured in the United States of America
Cover Design: Jenny Buono
Interior Design: Tim Holtz

Walking Together, Finding the Way
Published by SkyLight Paths Publishing
A Division of LongHill Partners, Inc.
An Imprint of Turner Publishing Company
4507 Charlotte Avenue, Suite 100
Nashville, TN 37209
Tel: (615) 255-2665
www.skylightpaths.com

To Hari Kirin

Contents

Introduction to Gospel

Why a New Translation?

In my travels I have met many people who grew up hearing the Gospels in church and have now moved on in a different direction. Some have found their religion outmoded or just do not feel like participating any longer. Some have been offended, like many women who find formal religion sexist. Others are attracted to altogether different traditions, and some do not see the point of religion at all.

Many told me they missed the stories and the teachings, and wished they could have a better, more up-to-date understanding of them. I have heard from other people who did not have a Christian background and wondered if the Gospels could add to their more open-ended spiritual path. I have strong empathy for both positions and wanted to present the Gospels in a way that would speak to both.

Some Christians, both traditional and independent, expressed their fervent curiosity about how I might understand the teachings, given my unusual background as a monk, a student of world religions, and a depth psychotherapist. I felt their eagerness and sincerity when they asked me to recommend a good translation. I could not direct them without reservation to any translation that I knew and trusted, so the idea of my own version took root.

Another reason I felt it was time for a new version was my frustration at seeing faulty religious ideas, specifically about the teachings of Jesus, dragging down important political advances in our society. You do not have to look far beneath the headlines to see uninformed, emotional, and sentimental notions of Jesus's philosophy. Today we cannot afford to keep referring to outmoded and faulty versions of Jesus's teachings and using them to support questionable causes.

In the end, I wanted to make the Gospels accessible and attractive to all sorts of readers. I see no indication that Jesus intended to create a religion or a church. His purpose is clear: He wanted to raise human awareness and behavior to another level, where it would surpass its tendencies toward self-interest, xenophobia, greed, religious moralism, and an emphasis on insignificant rules. He imagined a more just and pleasurable world, a "kingdom of the sky." He was explicit in instructing his students to speak to everyone, not just some particular and chosen religious group.

In my translation there is no suggestion that readers should believe in anything, join an organization, or abandon their cherished religious and philosophical ideals. I see no reason why a Christian, an agnostic, a Buddhist, or even an atheist would not be charmed and inspired by the Gospels. Anyone can freely and without any worries read the Gospels and be enriched.

These texts are sacred not because they belong to a particular religion or spiritual tradition but because they offer a vision and a way of life that transcends the limits of reason and will. They show a figure in love with life and with a heart open to all sorts of people, but at the same time a figure constantly in tune with the Sky Father, that image of ultimate transcendence that provides an opening, a tear in the fabric of human consciousness, a doorway to the infinite and the eternal.

The Gospels are not just books of practical wisdom—how to live more effectively. They are also books of mysteries, assuming that to be fully human we have to open ourselves to the mysterious depth and height of the world that is our home.

Who Was Jesus?

It is a simple question, isn't it? Who was Jesus? But the debate over the historical Jesus was been raging for at least two centuries. There is not much factual material to go on, and though the Gospels often sound like biography or history, clearly they are largely stories told to evoke a religious milieu. Historically, they are full of contradictions and gaps and fantasy material. This does not make them worthless in themselves. On the contrary, they are marvelous, simply ingenious inventions for spiritual teaching, but as history they are unreliable, to say the least.

It appears that Jesus was born around 4 BCE, when Romans were occupying the Mediterranean area of Jesus's birth and travels. Herod the Great was king, having been put in place by the Romans. Greek language and culture were strong in the area, and Egypt, with its colorful past and rich spiritual culture, was not far away. There is evidence of a temple to the Greek god Dionysus in Jesus's area, and yet he was also dealing daily with Jewish teachings, customs, and rules. The Gospels portray many verbal skirmishes between Jesus and leaders, religious and social, who spoke up for Jewish law and tradition.

Jesus taught in the synagogues and to some appeared to be the long-awaited Messiah, the anointed leader of a new Jewish order. Many events and sayings in the Gospels echo Hebrew Bible writings, suggesting a layer of Messiah in Jesus's words and actions. But this aspect also casts a shadow on Jesus's presence and work, leading to the notion that he was "king of the Jews" and therefore a threat to Roman, local, and religious authority. Jesus was executed somewhere around 30 BCE, perhaps in his early thirties.

It is often said that people who read the Gospels see the Jesus they want to see. Some understand him to be a religious reformer, some a social rebel, and some the founder of a religious tradition. He is sometimes described as a teacher of wisdom, a label that comes close to my own view but is not quite serious enough. I see him more as a social mystic, like a shaman who can heal and lead people to appreciate multiple layers of their reality.

At his baptism, the sky opens and the Sky Father speaks favorably of him, blessing him essentially. For me, this is a key moment, because Jesus is forever talking about his father in the sky, recommending that we always live in relation to that transcendent realm as well as in the present moment where our goodwill and powers of healing are always needed.

Jesus also has a relation to the dead, and his own death is always looming. So in the end we have a Jesus who as shaman and mystic speaks and acts from the plane of daily life, from the transcendent level of the Father, and in the realm of the dead. This is more than lessons in practical wisdom. It is a profound mystical vision that combines social action, based on the principle of friendship and not just altruism, and an all-embracing mystical awareness of timeless realities and sensibilities.

Some think that Jesus wanted to create a religion or a church. Some think he was often speaking about the afterlife. In my translation and commentary, I move in a different direction. I think he was trying to convince people to live

in an entirely different way, with basic values of love and community instead
of self-interest and conflict. He suggested keeping the highest ideals in mind
instead of merely trying to amass money and possessions. He spoke and acted
contrary to moralistic laws and customs and showed in his manner of living
that friends and good company were worth more than pious activities. He told
all his students to be healers and to help people rid themselves of compulsive
behaviors. Above all, he suggested that we get over all the artificial boundaries
set up between religions and cultures and live as though we were all brothers
and sisters. "Who is my family?" (Matthew 12:48), he asks, and he points to the
students and others gathered around him.

What Is a Gospel?

The story of Jesus's life and teachings was written down, after a fairly long
period of oral storytelling, by many writers, each having a different purpose.
We get the essentials of the story in Mark, strong references to Jewish tradition
in Matthew, important elaboration of the stories and teachings in Luke, and a
mystical dimension in John. By the fifth century CE, the church had made these
four versions official. They are called "canonical," the only ones approved by
the church at that time: Matthew, Mark, Luke, and John. These writings first
appeared somewhere between 65 CE and 110 CE, at least thirty-five years after
Jesus's death. The book of Mark was the oldest, and the writers of Matthew and
Luke took some material from Mark.

So think about that—a teacher appears and dies, and decades later a few
devotees write down some stories about his life and try to capture his teachings,
based on what had been passed down by word of mouth. Besides problems with
memory, the various stories, as we see in the canonical Gospels, conveyed a different sense of what Jesus was all about. They were interpretations, not histories.

Two millennia later, modern people try to make sense of these written doc-
uments. Not being historians, they tend to take the stories as plain fact and
even try to live by their interpretations. Some of the tales are quite fantastic:
miraculous healings, raising the dead to life, the teacher himself surviving death,
miraculous meals, and angels appearing here and there. Put together these two
aspects—fantastic events and a tendency to take every word literally—and you
have problems in understanding.

Strictly speaking, the word "Gospel" in the original Greek means "good message." It has been translated as "good news" or "glad tidings," both accurate and beautiful phrases. But what is the good news? That is not so easy to sort out.

The Translation

If you have grown up reading the Gospels or hearing them read in church, you may think that the translation you take for granted is official or sacred. But the Gospels were originally written in a form of Greek spoken by people in everyday life. Historians generally agree that Jesus spoke Aramaic and that the Gospels were written in Greek. There is no widely accepted ancient Aramaic version, though some think that the Greek Gospels, in particular Matthew and Luke, may have been based on Aramaic sources.

If you were to read the Gospels in the original Greek, you would be surprised, maybe even shocked, to see how simple the language is. The vocabulary is limited, and many sentences read almost like a book meant for children. The Book of Luke is somewhat more sophisticated than Mark, and Matthew lies in the middle. But still the Greek is quite plain. This means that a translator has great liberty in using a number of different words for the simple ones that keep coming up and is likely to infuse his version with his own biases and points of view.

In rendering the Greek Gospels into English, I would like to have come up with astonishing, florid, and entrancing phrases. But, as I said, the original is so simple that it would be a travesty to make it too elaborate. I had two principles in mind as I made this translation: I wanted to give the reader a version that would flow gracefully and be as clear and limpid as I could make it, and I wanted to use striking new English words for a few key terms that I thought were usually misunderstood.[1] I worked hard to be sure that my versions of these words had the backing of history and scholarship.

Jesus as Poet

I see Jesus as a spiritual poet. There is a striking passage in the Book of Matthew where his students are being literal and he corrects them. Matthew comments, "He said nothing to the people that was not a parable" (Matthew 13:34). By "poet" I do not mean that he speaks or writes poetry, but that he uses narrative and imagery to get his rich ideas across. He does not speak like an academic or a theologian, defining his terms and setting out his ideas pedantically. He is part teacher and part entertainer, a spiritual leader and a bard, a shaman and an enchanter.

A spiritual poet uses language for its beauty and for the power of its imagery. He wants to give the listener or reader insight into life. A poet does not force an understanding of life or an ideology onto his listeners. His narratives and images are meant to deepen a person's view of life. Some topics disappear in highly rationalistic language, while a more imagistic approach better conveys the mysteries involved.

If Jesus says that he speaks in parables, we should have a good idea about what a parable is. People often think of a parable as a simple, moral teaching story. But scripture scholar Robert Funk says that a parable helps us "cross over" into the mysterious land that Jesus is trying to evoke for us, a kingdom in which life is radically different. Similarly, the renowned scholar John Dominic Crossan says that a parable "shatters our complacency" and pulls us out of the comfortable picture of life we have always lived by.

A parable is the opposite of a gentle teaching story. It confronts us, asking us to change our way of seeing things. It turns conventional ideas upside down. Its very point is to make us uncomfortable. In plain teaching in the Book of Matthew, Jesus says, "Love your enemies and speak well of those who criticize you. This way you can become sons of your father in the sky. For he makes the sun rise on the bad and the good and rain on the just and the unjust" (Matthew 5:44–45).

For many, this teaching is just too radical. How many people show any love for those they consider enemies? Later he tells the parable of a woman who hid a small amount of yeast in a large pile of flour. That is what the Jesus kingdom is like. It is not overt, not even visible, and it is tiny. Yet it can change a life and alter the course of the world. If only a small portion of people in the world understood that somehow you have to love your enemies, we might not go on dividing ourselves into the good and the bad, and the Jesus vision would gain some traction.

Much of what is written in the Gospels is poetic in style, sometimes metaphorical and allegorical. You have to have a sharp and sophisticated appreciation for symbol and image or you might completely misread the text.

For example, Jesus heals a blind man. Is this a simple miraculous good deed or does it speak to a less literal blindness? Do we all fail to see life for what it is and have the wrong view of our place in the world? The Gospel writer himself speaks about this more poetic kind of blindness.

A Better Word for "Sin"

Many translations of the Gospels have a moralistic air. The translator may think of Christianity as a religion of do's and don'ts, and that point of view leads him to translate certain words with a heavy moral slant. Take the word "sin," so often used in English versions. Many readers of the Gospels know that the word originally meant "off the mark." Yet we do not use the word "sin" that way. We mean that someone has done something so bad that it merits everlasting punishment. As a child growing up in a devout Catholic family, I was always being told, "Don't do that. You'll go to hell." What if an adult had said to me, "There you go again. You're off the mark. You need to get your values straight." At least I would have had a chance to do better.

I do not translate the Greek word *hamartia* as "sin" or even "off the mark." I prefer the reflections of the pre-Christian philosopher Aristotle, who in his book on poetry and drama, *Poetics*, discusses the role of *hamartia* in tragedy. He says it refers to an action done out of ignorance that has tragic consequences.

When I was a child, I had a BB gun and shot some birds. I still feel remorse for doing such a thing. I needed to be taught the value of innocent animal life. My ignorance led me to actions I now regret. I would not say that I committed a sin, but that in my ignorance I made a mistake that today I mourn. I do not consider myself a horrible person and carry that guilt with me, but I understand that I have to keep learning and become more aware so I do not make worse mistakes.

With Aristotle's thoughtful explanation in mind, how would you translate *hamartia*? It is complicated. Maybe several words would be better than one. I tend to use the word "mistake," but I know that alone it sounds too weak. Usually I qualify it according to the context in which it is used. I do not want to imply that *hamartia* is a simple, everyday misstep, but neither do I want to suggest high-minded moralistic judgment, which I do not pick up from the Gospels in Greek. So I often used the phrase "tragic mistake."

I have seen many English translations of the Gospels that try to make the language more modern in style than the familiar, often archaic renditions. I appreciate many of these modern versions, but none interprets the Gospels the way I do. I have my own idea of what the Gospels are about, and my translation expresses that viewpoint. "Sin" is only one of many key words that affect the way we understand what Jesus was up to and what he taught. Not finding "sin" in this translation, I hope you read the Gospels without beating yourself up for having done wrong. I hope you see that Jesus was not moralistic but rather deeply concerned about the roots of self-serving and destructive behavior.

Some Key Images

For years in writing many books I have turned to Greek classical literature for insight, especially the great tragedies and comedies, the hymns to the gods and goddesses, and the mythological stories. In the Gospel translation, whenever I come across any connection between the Gospels and these classical sources I take note of the crossover and see if it offers any special insight. In some cases, the parallels are striking and in others subtle and hidden. In general, an awareness of earlier uses of Greek terms helps us understand better what is being said in the Gospels.

As a student of both religion and depth psychology, I have spent many years studying Greek polytheism. I have been amazed by the richness, complexity, and insightfulness of the ancient tales of the gods and goddesses. If you were to read some of the penetrating essays by my mentor James Hillman or the well-known mythologist Joseph Campbell, you would see how the old Greek stories help us gain insight into the patterns and dynamics of our everyday lives.

As I was poring over the Greek text of the Gospels, studying one key word after another, I discovered several instances in which a reference to one of the ancient Greek stories lay buried in the etymology or structure of the word.

The Kingdom of the Sky

The clearest example is the phrase "kingdom of heaven" or "our father who art in heaven." The Greek word usually translated as "heaven" is *ouranos*. The word could be taken as an ordinary term for the sky, but it is also the exact name for the sky-god of the Greeks, Ouranos, today usually spelled Uranus, like the planet.

When I read the words "kingdom of heaven" (*ouranos*), I am inclined to translate it as "kingdom of the sky." I will say more about this image later, but my point here is that the Greek version of the Gospels has layers, and, whether intended or not, deep themes peek through and enrich the stories and teachings.

The Kingdom

You get the sense in the Gospels that Jesus is an intimate and special son of the Sky Father. The kingdom he is creating on earth is a way of life sanctioned by this father. When asked how to pray, Jesus says, "Say, our father in the sky, may your name be held sacred...."

I see the sky as a metaphor, or better yet, an archetypal image. Its meaning is based on ordinary experience: You look at the sky at night or even during the day, and you may wonder about the meaning of everything and your place in life. You may imagine other worlds, other planets, and other civilizations. You may look into the light-blue daytime heavens or the blue-black night and sense infinity and eternity. The kingdom of the sky, therefore, is not like practical, factual, and self-absorbed life. It is an alternative, the object of wonder and perfection, eternal and infinite. The "father" of that realm offers a more perfected idea of what human life could be.

The kingdom of the sky comprises those people who live the values Jesus specifies in his teaching, especially the one about respecting any person who is not of your circle. Jesus does not talk about love as a sentimental emotion. That is why I usually translate *agape* as "respect." If your basic motivation in all of life is love and respect, you are automatically in the kingdom. But take note: Jesus makes it clear that your actions have to follow your values in this regard.

The Sky and the Sky Father

I prefer to use the word "sky" instead of "heaven" because it is a concrete image. I do not mean a literal father in the clouds but rather the sky as an image for spirit. As I have read the passages about the Sky Father, I have had in mind the Native American mystic Black Elk, praying to the parents and grandparents in the sky.

Here is a typical passage from Black Elk that influenced me in translating *Ouranos*:

> The fifth Grandfather spoke, the oldest of them all, The Spirit of the Sky. "My boy," he said, "I have sent for you and you have come. My power you shall see!" He stretched his arms and turned into a spotted eagle hovering. "Behold," he said, "all the wings of the air shall come to you, and they and the winds and the stars shall be like relatives. You shall go across the earth with my power." Then the eagle soared above my head and fluttered there; and suddenly the sky was full of friendly wings all coming toward me.[2]

This passage has much in common with the Gospels, as when Jesus is baptized and the father speaks from the sky and the spirit appears as a hovering dove. The Gospel describes the sky as sometimes full of not wings but angels—close.

Hesiod, one of the early Greek spiritual poets, describes "Ouranos"—the word used every time for Gospel phrases like "kingdom of the sky" and "our father in the heavens"—this way:

> *The first one born of Gaia (Earth) was Ouranos.*
> *He was as big as she was.*
> *He was the sky full of stars.*
> *He spread over her*
> *and was*
> *a solid ground for the holy immortals.*

You can pray to the father, as Jesus did, and yet know that you are addressing something mysterious and vastly spiritual. Our usual anthropomorphic—human-like—language is only an approximation of the sublime mystery of this father. As the spirit of the sky, he is the "ground for the holy immortals" or, we might say, "the ground for our spiritual vision."

The kingdom of the sky or the heavens is a place set apart because of its special values and the primacy of its rule of love and respect, *agape*. Jesus wants neither the rule-bound religion of the church officials nor the self-satisfied realm of the purely secular. He calls for a third alternative, a place where you can live a life based on spiritual values of love and respect.

The Commentary

Because there are so many words of such complexity in the Gospels, I have included many notes on the translation and comments on the meaning. Some of them come from other sources, offering either an expert reflection on the passage or special insight from an artist. From the beginning I wanted to include comments from thinkers of many different spiritual traditions. Why not? Their different perspectives open up fresh ways of understanding the Gospel stories and teachings. I try to set aside my own academic interests and get to the heart of the matter. If I mention an expert or a writer from history, like Aristotle's thoughts about mistakes, or a poet like Anne Sexton, I do not call on them as authorities, as though I were writing a school paper. I mention them because their brilliant ideas are relevant. I hope that their way of seeing the issue will enrich your reading of the Gospels.

Most of the time my comments are my own take on the passage in question. A friend advised me on this project: "People aren't going to read your version because you're a scholar or have a mind-blowing translation to offer. They'll want to know what you think about the various stories and teachings. They want to know your ideas because you write about the soul and how to live more deeply and with less conflict." I heard what he said and beefed up my own commentary.

I want to open up the Gospel message by showing how people of various traditions and expertise interpreted certain passages. I quote Christian, Jewish, Sufi, Buddhist, and secular writers; poets, politicians, theologians, and Bible experts. Then I bring my own point of view to various passages, basing my reflections on my studies in depth psychology, world religions, mythology, and the arts. I rely on decades of experience as a psychotherapist, and I am aware of my own development in relation to the Gospels, from my childhood, when I heard them naively; to my monastic days, when I studied them in a Christian context; to now, when I blend the sacred and secular in everything I do and when I am always the psychotherapist. I could make a case that Jesus was a psychotherapist, and, in fact, the word "therapy" is often used in the Greek version to denote Jesus as a healer.

I think that the deeper point of the Gospels has been lost over the years, when people have focused on them as a source of strict moral lessons and the cornerstones for belief, and the establishment of a religion, church, or spiritual community. To me, Jesus says clearly that he is speaking to everyone who will listen, and his message has sophisticated psychological insight. My intention with the commentary is to release the Gospels from their narrow confinements and show how valuable they are today to anyone at all looking for insight into how to live deeply and lovingly.

The Gospels Are for Everyone

Returning to a close study of the Gospels has helped me personally with my spiritual life. These texts now inspire me more forcefully than at any time in my life. I do not see them as representing or advocating a particular religious viewpoint but as setting out a way of life, a secular set of values, that could help humanity survive and thrive. While I certainly do not want to convert anyone to a particular religion or church, I would like to see the whole world adopt this vision for humanity, based on love, respect, healing, and compassion.

I hope this new translation will move us in a more thoughtful, subtle, and compassionate direction in our own way of living and in our attitude toward others, especially those different from us. This is a key part of Jesus's teachings: He is forever telling people to love those who are outside their own circle. The kingdom is for them, he says, not for the in crowd.

My own practice is to keep at hand several different translations of sacred texts. I have seven versions of the Tao Te Ching on my shelves close at hand. I recommend doing the same with the Gospels. For example, I have relied on the beautiful translation by the Jesus Seminar in a book called *The Acts of Jesus.* I respect the scholarship behind that translation, though I did not want to use such complicated language in my own version. I admire the witty and profound translations of certain passages by John Dominic Crossan in his book *The Essential Jesus.* "The somebodies will be nobodies and the nobodies will be somebodies." You cannot get a better translation than that.

If you are looking for a more extravagant version or something completely different, those translations are available. But if you want an accurate version that is close to the original in vocabulary and tone, presented in simple, rhythmic English, then mine might do. If you want help understanding the sometimes difficult passages, not from a scholar's point of view but from someone with a background in depth psychology, literature, and world religions, then you may want to add this one to your collection.

It is my conviction that the less literally you take most passages, the more you will be inspired to live an altogether different kind of life, one in which your heart is more open than you ever thought it could be. You will have found a kind of utopia, an island of meaning radically different from the one that rules the world today. You can live this way now and find joy and substance in your life. And you can promote it as a way for the future—not a belief system or a church or religion, but a way of being in the world, open and radically accepting.

Introduction to the Book of Matthew

The Book of Matthew was written somewhere between 80 and 90 CE, not by the apostle but by an unknown writer who drew from the Book of Mark, a collection of Jesus's sayings known as "Q," and another collection of sayings known as "M." "M" contains teachings special to the editor given the honorific name of the apostle Matthew. Though the Book of Mark is the older document, the Book of Mathew usually comes first, both because at one time it was thought to be the oldest Gospel and because it has had the reputation of being the most important in terms of content.

One of the real strengths of the Book of Matthew is its paradoxical way of relating Jesus's main teachings and actions to Hebrew Bible models and then suggesting that these teachings belong to the whole world, including the pagan world. Just after Jesus dies, a Roman soldier says, "He must have been a son of God." The Gospels have the subtlety of novels; images and phrases suggest more than what appears there. This statement from the mouth of a centurion picks up a common theme in the Gospels: Jesus's followers often turn out to be those we least expect.

With similar literary skill, Matthew presents Jesus as a new Moses. Jesus is a leader of great spiritual significance, born in circumstances that echo those of Moses and delivering his key teaching, his new commandments, in his sermon on the mountain, reminding the reader of the Ten Commandments and Mount Sinai.

In my own reading of this Gospel, the heart of the matter comes at Matthew 10:7–8, when Jesus sends the apostles out to do their work, following his example:

> *The kingdom is drawing near.*
> *Care for those who are suffering.*
> *Wake up those who are unconscious.*

Refresh those who have suffered.
Get rid of daimonic tendencies.

This passage gives a five-point set of instructions for both the apostles and the reader today. This is how you live the Gospel teaching. You are aware that an altogether new way of living is just around the corner. You can do it easily, if you look closely at the teachings and Jesus's example. But you need a utopian frame of mind, because the Jesus kingdom is not life as usual. It is not self-centered and not achieved at the expense of anyone else. Jesus's words and example offer a different way to live your life.

The first statement about the kingdom sets up the situation: Get ready for a new way of doing things. Next—and this is the basic operating principle—care for those who are suffering. Here the key word in Greek is *therapeia*, a form of "therapy." If you understood the word deeply, the way Plato and other Greek thinkers did, you could translate this instruction, "Do therapy for those who are suffering." You often read, "Heal the sick." But in Greek, *therapeia* is always either "care" or "service." For too long we have thought of Jesus as a miracle worker, rather than a spiritual teacher showing what we should all do—care for the sick and the disturbed.

The next duty is to wake up those who are unconscious. "Wake up" is one of the key phrases in the Gospels. If you want to follow the Jesus way, the Tao of Jesus, you must yourself wake up and help others to do the same. We see the same emphasis in Buddhism. The Buddha is the Awakened One, and students sometimes need a jolt of enlightenment, which is another way of saying awakening.

The next instruction is somewhat more subtle: "Refresh those who have suffered." The word here is *catharsis*, "cleansing." People who suffer in various ways are often rejected and ostracized. They need to have their dignity and sense of belonging to the community restored. In the Gospels you see Jesus treating everyone, but especially the rejected, with extraordinary respect. As a psychotherapist, I would say that healing begins with the restoration of respect, and I always do my best to show deep respect for people in their moments of confusion and suffering. It is the base of good therapy, and we find it among the fundamental instructions of Jesus to his apostles. Among other things, Jesus is a very savvy therapist.

The last equally challenging demand is to get rid of daimonic tendencies. The Greek word is *daimonia*. You could translate it as "demons," as in to "cast out demons," but *daimon* is different. It means any urge, instinct, or drive that compels us to act unconsciously and often destructively without having much control. There is no question that one of the greatest threats to relationships, personal tranquillity, and social peace is daimonic acting out. We see it in excessive patriotism, violent anger, and sexual domination.

The figure of Jesus is not one of passive calm but rather of someone who knows how to relate to the *daimon* when it appears. His tranquillity comes from having dealt with the daimonic in life rather than avoiding it. He enjoys the strength of self-possession, and this quality is so important that he includes it in his instructions to his apostles as they set out into the world with the aim of establishing the new, utopian kingdom.

There are hints of a similar psychological complexity in the genealogy that Matthew lists at the beginning of his Gospel account. Clearly, the purpose of the genealogy is to give Jesus his place in the lineage from Abraham and down through David. This descending line prepares us for Jesus's birth at Bethlehem. It is a long list of male names, but among them are five women, if you include Mary, the mother of Jesus.

These women are sometimes known as the "grandmothers," and it is interesting that none of them is a model of moral perfection and faith. Tamar seduces Judah and gives birth to Perez, who is on the list. Rahab is a prostitute and the first gentile with faith in the God of Israel. She is the mother of Boaz, who marries Ruth, a Moabite, who chooses the faith of Naomi, her Jewish mother-in-law. Ruth is David's great-grandmother. The wife of Uriah is Bathsheba, with whom David has an affair and whose husband he kills. Their child is Solomon.

That leads us to Mary, the mother of Jesus. We understand her today to be spotless, but the story points out that her husband thought of divorcing her because of her pregnancy. So even Mary has a spotted story to tell.

I wonder if the lives of these complicated women give us a proper introduction to Jesus, who was accused of hanging around with disreputable people. As playwright Oscar Wilde notes, "He [Jesus] regarded sin and suffering as being in themselves beautiful, holy things, and modes of perfection."[1] Jesus wanted people to wake up and live by a philosophy of radical love, but his followers were earthy people and he passed up opportunities to moralize against people who were prostitutes or occupying soldiers. His utopian kingdom is not without basic human complexity.

It is a pleasure to read Matthew's artful, layered, and intelligent portrayal of Jesus. But you have to think in layers and metaphors and cannot be simplistic when you read him. Nor should you think of Jesus as a one-dimensional figure. His teachings and his life present us with a challenge today, because we have to consider seriously and concretely how to establish utopia, the sky kingdom, on earth.

THE BOOK OF
MATTHEW

Chapter 1

The genealogical record of Jesus Christos,
the son of David, the son of Abraham.

Abraham
Isaac
Jacob
Judah and his brothers
Judah the father of Perez and Zerah
Tamar
Perez the father of Hezron
Ram
Amminadab
Hahshon
Salmon
Salmon the father of Boaz
Rahab
Boaz the father of Obed
Ruth
Obed
Jesse
King David
Solomon
Uriah's wife
Rehoboam
Abijah
Asa
Jehoshaphat
Jehoram
Uzziah
Jotham

1 "Matthew traces Jesus'[s] lineage from Abraham by way of King David,
thereby establishing as a descendant of David and therefore 'the Anointed'
or messiah."
    —Robert Funk and the Jesus Seminar, *The Acts of Jesus: What Did Jesus Really Do?*
    (Salem, OR: Polebridge Press, 1998), 500

Ahaz

Hezekiah

Manasseh

Amon

Josiah

Jeconiah (and his brothers at the time of the exile to Babylon)

Shealtiel

Zerubbabel

Abiud

Eliakim

Azor

Zadok

Akim

Eliud

Eleazar

Matthan

Jacob

Joseph, the husband of Mary, of whom was born Jesus called Christos.

And so there were fourteen generations from Abraham to David, fourteen from David to the exile in Babylon, and fourteen from the exile to Christos.[1]

2   The Greek has no capital letters. The usual proper name "Holy Spirit" can be misleading. Throughout the stories of the Gospels you will come across "a holy spirit" that is a creative influence on events. This is a real, felt experience: having a holy spirit come into you and change you and redirect your destiny.

3   Jesus has two fathers: an earthly one and a father above. He has two ways of being—one a very human earthly life and the other fully placed in the eternal and spiritual. But we all have these two natures, worldly and spiritual. We all need an ordinary fathering and an invisible guidance.

This is how the birth of Jesus unfolded:

His mother Mary was engaged to Joseph, but before they slept together, she became pregnant by a holy spirit.[2] Joseph was a considerate man and didn't want to disgrace her publicly. So he thought he would break up with her quietly.

But just as he had made his decision, one of the Lord's angels showed up in a dream and said, "Don't worry about Mary and this marriage. She has become pregnant by a holy spirit. She'll give birth to a son, and you'll name him Jesus, and he will help people avoid making tragic mistakes."

All of this fulfilled what the Lord had said through his prophet:

> *The virgin will get pregnant and give birth to a son and they'll give him the name Emmanuel, "God among us."*

When Joseph woke up, he did what the Lord's angel told him to do. He went ahead with the marriage to Mary. But he didn't sleep with her until she gave birth to a son. They named him Jesus.[3]

1   Herod the Great (74 BCE–4 CE), a cruel tyrant in the service of the Romans, was known for his grand building projects and his unbridled quest for power.

2   *Magi* is the plural of *magus*. These were people skilled in astrology, magic symbols and lore, curses and blessings, and all-around magical skills. Today we do not generally accept real *magi* in our midst and perhaps find it difficult to imagine how significant it is in this story that *magi* come to honor the birth of Jesus. But, more than any others, they could appreciate his powers of healing and persuasion, for persuasion is a magic art, too.

3   Since the *magi* are talking, they may well be referring to an astrological omen. This passage suggests that we think astrologically about the Gospels and always recognize a cosmic dimension in them. These simple stories are about an effort to transform the very world in which we live. A spiritual vision carries us off into the vast universe, where we can better understand the sublime aspects of being human.

    Jesus is a *magus*, in a way. He works magic with his stories and healing, and he invites us to cultivate this aspect of life as well. But we often think of magic as superstitious and ancient, belonging to a time past, or as New Age, too precious and full of tricks. Look carefully and notice how Jesus manifests his power and consider that real magic is at work in his teaching and his healings. If you are interested in exploring Jesus as *magus*, see Morton Smith's *Jesus the Magician: Charlatan or Son of God?* (Berkeley, CA: Ulysses Press, 1998).

Chapter 2

A fter Jesus was born in Judea in the little hamlet of Bethlehem during the reign of Herod,¹ magicians² from the East
traveled to Jerusalem and made inquiries, "Where is the child-
king of the Jews?" We saw his star ascending³ and have come
to celebrate him." When King Herod heard about this he was
deeply disturbed, and everyone in Jerusalem felt his anxiety.

He brought together the spiritual leaders and the best legal
minds and asked them where Christos would be born. "In Bethlehem of Judea," they answered. The prophet had written:

Bethlehem, you're an important town in Judah. A leader
will come from your borders and shepherd my people
Israel.

4 In his fascinating essay "The Star of the Magi," fifteenth-century Italian scholar and philosopher Marsilio Ficino describes this star as an angel. The angel compacts or squeezes the air around itself into a tightly compressed comet of light, made up of its own intelligence. According to Ficino, when the angel appears in a dream, it comes on hidden rays, and as a star it is present through visible rays. This theory of the angel star may seem quaint and naive but it deserves consideration. It is not naive to think of an angel as a real being in the imaginal realm (*mundus imaginalis*), somewhere between the physically real and the purely imaginary, or as a fantastic being with direct relevance to our human experience.

5 "Myrrh was used as the sacred incense during the festival of Adonis. In some myths [Adonis] was said to have been born from a myrrh tree. In others his mother is named Myrrh.

"Jesus was born in the little town of Bethlehem, meaning 'The House of Bread.' St. Jerome mentions that Bethlehem was shaded by a grove sacred to the Mystery god-man Adonis, who was regarded as a god of the grain and represented by bread."

—Timothy Freke and Peter Gandy, *The Jesus Mysteries: Was the "Original Jesus" a Pagan God?* (New York: Three Rivers Press, 1999), 33

6 The Gospels emphasize the role of dreams, suggesting that we, too, could approach dreams seriously as a guide to life. Today, many people seem interested in dreams and express a desire to know more about them. You could read about dreams in the Gospels and decide to include dreamwork in your own Gospel-style practice.

7 It might be helpful to remember the association of angels and dreams. You may think of angels as real, just as dreams are real and significant. But their kind of reality is not the same as going to lunch or cleaning your house. The Sufi scholar Henri Corbin calls it *mundus imaginalis*, the imaginal realm. This is not an imaginary place but a world that comes into being when you take images seriously and appreciate the reality of things that are not physical and yet perceptible and meaningful.

8 Hosea 11:1.

Herod summoned the magicians and ascertained the precise time the star had appeared. Then he sent them to Bethlehem, encouraging them to make a careful search for the child. "When you find him, let me know. I'd like to go and celebrate his birth, too."

They listened to the king and then continued on their journey. The star they had seen rising went in front of them and then paused over the place where the child was.[4] When they noticed the star come to a stop, they were overjoyed. They went into the shelter and beheld the child with his mother Mary and bowed down in honor and opened their chests and offered him gifts of gold, incense, and myrrh.[5] Warned in a dream not to return to Herod, they took another route back home.[6]

When they had gone, an angel of the Lord spoke to Joseph in a dream,[7] "Get up, take mother and child and escape to Egypt and stay there until I tell you differently. Herod will be on the lookout for the child to kill him." So Joseph got up and took the mother and child to Egypt and stayed there until Herod's death. This fulfilled what the Lord had said through the voice of a prophet:

Out of Egypt I have called my son.[8]

9   Jeremiah 31:15. Later we will see that the kingdom of the sky is in many ways a child's world, a place of loving care. King Herod's massacre of children is a particularly harsh sign that the kingdom will be rejected by those in power and that its opponents may be brutally antichild. The power-world of ordinary reality not only rejects the importance of the child but is also outright antagonistic toward children. Many appreciate the innocence of childhood but others find it annoying, naive, and even threatening. Jesus recommends starting over, being born once again into a different world, being more like a child than an adult.

10 Archelaus was one of Herod the Great's sons. His father made him his successor, but only of a third of the kingdom. He is not known precisely as king but rather ethnarch. He was educated in Rome and later closely monitored by Augustus in Rome.

11 Here we have two significant themes: protecting the child and turning to dreams for guidance. Later, Jesus will tell his followers to bring children to him because they belong in the kingdom. Here we see the child safeguarded. We could generalize and say that to follow the spirit of the Gospels we should do everything possible to protect children. We also see that dreams are not just interesting images to be interpreted but also messages to follow with close attention and trust.

When Herod saw that the magicians had tricked him, he went into a rage and ordered all boys in Bethlehem and its surroundings two and under to be killed. He figured out the timing from information the magicians had given him and thus fulfilled a saying from the prophet Jeremiah:

They heard a sound in Ramah—
weeping and loud lament,
Rachel weeping for her children
Because they are gone.[9]

After Herod had died and while the family was still in Egypt, an angel of the Lord appeared to Joseph in a dream and said, "Get up and take mother and child and go to the land of Israel. Those who wanted to kill the child are dead." So he got up and took mother and child to the land of Israel. But when he heard that Archelaus[10] was now ruling Judea in place of his father Herod, he was afraid to go there. Instead, he took the warning in the dream to heart and went to the Galilee area and lived in a village called Nazareth, once again fulfilling the prophets:[11]

They will call him a Nazarene.

1   "Era of the Sky Father" is usually translated "kingdom of heaven." The Greek
     word is *ouranos*, which means "sky" and also echoes the name of the ancient
     god of the Greeks, Ouranos, known by astrologers as Uranus. I imagine the
     kingdom from above as spirituality symbolized by the sky—vast, infinite,
     cosmic, at the very edge of our existence and dripping with the mystery that
     surrounds us. The more familiar translation, "heaven," suggests afterlife. I
     imagine instead that sense of wonder you feel when you contemplate either
     a day or a night sky, the Ouranos archetype. The sky sparks your imagina-
     tion to ask the big questions about life and death and symbolizes the full
     mystery that surrounds our lives. All human beings have a potentially rich
     and useful relationship to the sky. It affects our sense of who we are and what
     our destiny might be, and so it can symbolize great vision and idealism.

2   Isaiah 40:3.

3   This key word, *hamartias* in Greek, is usually translated as "sins." I say "fail-
     ings" to ease up on the moralistic tone usually given to the Gospels. Aristotle
     explained this word *hamartia* as the tragic situation in which a person makes
     a major mistake in life because of deep ignorance about what is happening
     around her. More popularly, the word is translated, in the context of Aristo-
     tle, as "fatal flaw." As many know, it also means "off the mark." "Sin" does not
     seem to be a good way to evoke any of these meanings.

4   One meaning of the word "baptize" is to dye by immersing a fabric in a col-
     ored liquid. This is a potential metaphor not used in the Gospels directly—
     changing color as an image for a change of heart.

Chapter 3

At that time John the Baptist was getting his message out in the wilderness areas of Judea: "Turn your life around. The era of the Sky Father[1] is drawing near."

The prophet Isaiah was thinking of John when he said,

The sound of someone
wailing in the wild:
"Make a path for the Lord
and keep the ground smooth."[2]

John wore clothes made of camel hair and had a leather belt around his waist and ate locusts and wild honey. People from Jerusalem and all of Judea and the entire region of the Jordan made the journey to see him. They acknowledged failings[3] and then he baptized[4] them in the Jordan River.

5   Pharisees were a Jewish sect at the time of Jesus. They promoted holiness and piety among Jews generally and believed in the resurrection of the dead. Some apparently supported Jesus and some argued against him.

Sadducees were a group of generally wealthy people who were somewhat conservative and did not believe in resurrection.

6   This challenge to do something constructive is a direct invitation to contribute to the change that Jesus teaches and exemplifies. It is a different way of life. You do not follow him only by using the actual words of the Gospels; you participate creatively and productively in changing the world. The key point in the Gospels is that it is possible to live life differently than normal. Some biblical experts refer to normal conditions as "default reality"—the world as it is before we apply the Jesus vision.

7   The image of trees being put into the fire comes up often. It is clear that in Jesus's teachings, if you do not live by the values of the kingdom, you will be lost and will suffer. Not choosing the kingdom is a bad option. Your choice either saves you or condemns you. Live violently and egotistically, and by that very choice you will be excluded from the healing, loving, and communal conditions of the new way of being.

8   Another key word: *metanoia*, in Greek; here translated as "change." It is often translated moralistically as "repentance." But the word consists of *meta*, as in "metamorphosis," a radical change, like the one from caterpillar to butterfly, and *noia*, "knowledge" or the order of the world. *Metanoia* is therefore a deep change in the way you understand the world. It refers to a shift in perception and being, as well as a change in the world in which you live. If we live the Gospel ideal, the culture will change. Imagination is the key, and the Gospels are all about a profound, life-altering shift in imagination. If you imagine life through the eyes of love, you are in quite a different world from one based on self-interest and aggression. To enjoy the new kingdom, you have to opt for a different way of life—opt, *metanoia*.

9   Another image of sorting and burning, and another reference to sorting the useful from the useless. Jesus draws a clear line between "things as usual" and "the new kingdom."

When he spotted several Pharisees and Sadducees[5] who had come for baptism, he said to them, "You sons of serpents! Who convinced you to ignore the sensibility that is coming into being? Do something constructive.[6] Don't just coddle each other by saying, 'We have our father Abraham.' I'm telling you, God can make children out of these stones for Abraham. Even now the ax lies at the trunk of the tree, and any tree that doesn't bear good fruit will be cut down and tossed into the fire.[7]

"I baptize you in the waters of change.[8] But later someone more powerful than me is coming. I'm not in a position even to carry his shoes. He will baptize you with a holy spirit and with fire. He is holding in his hand, so to speak, a tool for sifting grain. He'll clear his threshing floor, collect his wheat in the silo, and burn what's left."[9]

10 Discussing Plotinus, the originator of neoplatonism, a philosophy of soul, analytical psychologist Carl Jung says: "The mind thinks it up and the world-soul brings it to birth in the real world where it is drunk as if with nectar.... The intellect makes the soul fruitful. And the 'over-soul' is the heavenly Aphrodite, the 'undersoul' the earthly Aphrodite ... the dove of Aphrodite is the symbol of the Holy Ghost" (Jung).

Through the teachings and the image of the kingdom, Jesus offers a new level of intensity and spiritual intoxication symbolized by the Aphrodite dove. So, in Jung's view, the dove represents a feminine holy spirit, an erotic intensification of life, taught and exemplified by Jesus.

Around this time, Jesus left Galilee and joined John at the Jordan for his own baptism. Demurring, John said, "You should baptize me, and yet here you are."

Jesus responded, "That's all right. Let's do this and fulfill our obligations." John agreed.

After he was baptized, Jesus came up out of the water and the sky broke open and he saw a spirit of God come down like a dove and hover over him. [10] Then a sound rumbled in the sky, "This is my son. I love him dearly. He is a great blessing for me."

1   "[Jesus] is unlikely to have pronounced himself the Son of God, except in
    the sense that all the people of Israel were God's sons."
    —Michael Grant, *Jesus* (London: Weidenfeld and Nicolson, 1977), 172

    Notice, too, the image of bread, used frequently in the Gospels as a multi-
    tiered image of spiritual nourishment and the brotherhood and sisterhood of
    humanity. Jung lists four levels of meaning for bread and wine: "(1) as agri-
    cultural products; (2) as products requiring special processing (bread from
    grain, wine from grapes); (3) as expressions of psychological achievement
    (work, industry, patience, devotion, etc.) and of human vitality in general;
    (4) as manifestations of man or of the vegetation daimon" (Jung). Bread is
    also a vehicle for yeast, itself an image of how the kingdom works. It is a
    leavening factor, raising life to a new level.

2   This is a rather subtle reference to the kingdom: the difference between
    food for the body and food for the soul. If you are in the kingdom, you know
    that your soul, as well as your body, needs to be nourished. This is the first
    time we come across this central image of bread. The many references to
    it will culminate in the scene of the Last Supper, where bread becomes the
    main image for the presence of Jesus, his teaching, his community, and his
    ongoing influence.

3   There is something in human nature that loves miracles and superpowers.
    Here the temptation, one that might come to any of us, is to hold out for a
    miracle rather than live our humanity with spiritual and intellectual humil-
    ity. In the poetics of spiritual literature, miracles have an important place,
    but taken literally and then given too much importance, especially as proof
    of Jesus's divinity, they distort the meaning of the Gospels. Miracles give us
    images of how to live at the higher level shown in the Gospels.

Chapter 4

Then the spirit led Jesus out into the wild where the devil would test him. He fasted for forty days and forty nights and was hungry, so his challenger came up to him and said, "If you're a son of God, order these stones to become bread."[1]

"It's written," he said:

> "A human being lives not only on bread, but on every word that flows from the mouth of God."[2]

Then the devil led him to the holy city and stood him at the crown cornice of the temple and said, "If you are a son of God, jump. It's written:

> "He will order his angels to surround you and support you so you don't smash your foot on a stone."

Jesus said, "It's also written:

> "Don't put the Lord your God to the test."[3]

Once again the devil whisked him off in a visionary flight to a high mountain and showed him the nations of the earth in all their magnificence. "I'll give you all of this," he said, "if you bow down and adore me."

"Satan, back off, go away. It's also written:

> "The only one you should adore is the Lord your God. He is the one to worship."

Then the devil left him alone and angels came and looked after him.

4 Flavius Josephus (37 CE–c. 100 CE) was a Jewish scholar who wrote a history of the Jews in which he says that Herod Antipas, on the urging of his wife, imprisoned John the Baptist in Herod's fortress at Machaerus near the Dead Sea.

5 Isaiah 9:1–2.

6 This short sentence states a main theme of the Gospels, using three key concepts: *metanoia*, kingdom, and a warning that the kingdom is drawing near, almost in place, or about to be revealed. *Ouranos*, the Greek word I translate as "above," is the cosmic, divine context of our lives, the archetype of the sky. It is drawing near, perhaps because Jesus is presenting it as an option, not necessarily for the afterlife but for how we could live today. *Ouranos* is not literally otherworldly but it does suggest an alternative realm where values are more spiritual and visionary, maybe even utopian, not your usual worldly way of life, and therefore "above."

When Jesus heard that John had been put in prison,[4] he went off to Galilee, leaving Nazareth and staying in Capernaum near the sea, in the area of Zebulon and Naphthali, to fulfill what the prophet Isaiah had said:

> *Land of Zebulon and land of Naphthali,*
>> *the seaside route,*
>> *beyond the Jordan,*
>> *Galilee of the gentiles,*
> *The people who live in darkness*
>> *have seen a great light.*
>> *For those squatting in the gloom*
> *Of death's shadow*
>> *a light has risen.*[5]

From here on, Jesus's message became:

> *Change your life,*
> *because the kingdom of the father above*
> *is almost here.*[6]

7   Nets, fish, and fishermen play a significant symbolic role in the Gospels.
    The Greek lord of the Underworld was called Polydyktes, the man of many
    nets, and Jesus has been depicted as a fisherman of people as well as a fish.
    One thrust of the Gospels is to entice the whole world to live Jesus's val-
    ues (which is not the same as converting to Christianity). In his book *Aion:
    Researches into the Phenomenology of the Self*, Carl Jung offers many directions for
    exploring this theme. There he connects the many Gospel references to fish
    with the Pisces era, the Jesus epoch, a time when we can raise our lives to a
    new level of intimacy and community, thereby saving us from our destruc-
    tive habits. As fish, we might well be caught by Jesus, sailor and fisherman,
    and his inspiring spiritual vision.

8   The fishermen do not hesitate to leave their livelihood behind and imme-
    diately join up with Jesus. What immense charisma this little scene implies
    about the figure of Jesus. It suggests that we, too, can become inspiring peo-
    ple, charismatic and attractive in our approach to life. The Gospel way has a
    psychological impact, making you an outstanding person.

9   Caring for the sick and responding to suffering are central actions that
    define life in the kingdom. The traditional version of the Gospels usually
    emphasizes intellectual belief, but the Gospel texts teach healing, an action
    and not a belief, as the way to be a follower. Furthermore, the texts often
    imply that everyone needs healing, not only physically but also spiritually
    and emotionally.

Walking along the lake of Galilee, he saw two brothers—Simon, or Peter, and his brother Andrew. They were fishermen and were throwing a net into the water.[7] Jesus called out to them, "Come join me, fishermen, and let's catch some people." Without any hesitation they left their nets behind and followed him.[8]

Going on from there, he saw two other brothers: James and John, the sons of Zebedee. They were in a boat with their father Zebedee, working on the nets. He called out to them and they immediately left the boat and their father behind and became devoted to him.

Jesus traveled through Galilee, speaking in the synagogues, announcing the welcome news of the kingdom, and caring for people with all sorts of diseases and conditions. Word of him spread all over Syria. They brought him countless people suffering from a variety of illnesses—severe pain, psychogenic paralysis, and seizures—and he cared for them. Huge crowds from Galilee, the Decapolis, Jerusalem, Judea, and the area beyond the Jordan came to hear him.[9]

1   Here is another word with classical roots—*makarioi*. It refers to the place
    of bliss where the gods live and where people find deep happiness. The
    traditional translation "blessed" is perfectly fine, but "happy" seems closer to
    the word's nuances in Greek. "Like being in the presence of God" or "on the
    island of the immortals" would be more accurate but rather clumsy transla-
    tions. I am very tempted to say "In bliss are the poor in spirit."

2   The beatitudes are about the gift of bliss. The Gospels' hope is for a life of
    compassion that leads to a deep, communal happiness of a kind we have
    never seen before. Bliss is not superficial contentment but the joy that comes
    when you have a grounded yet positive view of life and find yourself in tune
    with it.

3   Salt is a key image for describing the kingdom. It is not a substance or food
    itself but a condiment, something that intensifies life and gives it flavor and
    zest. Psychologist James Hillman has written extensively on alchemical salt,
    or the salt of the psyche:

> The effect of salt proceeds from its own fervor, a fervor of fixity
> which can be distinguished from the fervor of sulphuric enthusiasm
> and its manic boil of action, as well as from the fervor of mercury and
> its effervescent volatilism. Salt's fervor is rather holy, cleansing, and
> bitter; immovably fixed; fanatic. (Jones, Jung, and Hillman)

Establishing and maintaining the kingdom in actual life, akin to the Buddhist
idea of nirvana, requires a salty fervor and intensity. Historically, we have
seen much fanaticism about believing and belonging to a church but not as
much fervor about establishing a world community and a neighborly way of
life. We have to be careful lest our salty enthusiasm turn into fanaticism, but
still, our devotion may be intense.

Chapter 5

As he watched the people gather in large groups, he went up a mountain and sat down and his followers came up, as well. Then he recited the beatitudes:

Happy[1] are the absolutely poor in spirit,
For them is the kingdom of the father above.
Happy are those who are grieving,
They'll be consoled.
Happy are the humble,
They will inherit the land.
Happy are those who hunger and thirst for equality,
They will be satisfied.
Happy are the compassionate,
They will find compassion.
Happy are the pure at heart,
They will see God.
Happy are the peacemakers,
They'll be known as children of God.
Happy are those abused for the sake of justice,
The kingdom is theirs.

"If people put you down and persecute you and lie about how terrible you are, all because of me, you, too, will be happy.[2]

"Be happy and joyful; your spiritual reward will be endless. Before you came, they persecuted the prophets when they spoke in this same way.

"You're the salt of the earth. But if the salt loses its tang, how can you restore it? It's no longer good for anything, so you toss it out and walk on it.[3]

4   Later, Jesus will tell us not to do good works just for show. Here he is saying that we should stand tall and not flaunt but boldly embody the great new philosophy of love and care. When people expect us to be worldly and cynical, we can fully embody the Jesus vision. People sometimes present this vision as though it were sentimental, too sweet and unreal. But it is a comprehensive approach to life that can be pursued with dignity and without apology.

5   Jesus was a gadfly, criticizing traditional religion; yet he clearly loved and honored his traditions. He sought to shift away from authoritarianism, meaningless rules, and pedantic interpretations. Accordingly, the Gospels can help you find deeper meaning in your own traditions, whatever they are.

6   "... to abide with the Holy is more fundamental than any case law and is itself original ethics and fundamental morality. It is also much more dangerous."
    —John Dominic Crossan, *Raid on the Articulate: Cosmic Eschatology in Jesus and Borges* (New York: Harper & Row, 1976), 69

Maybe this statement of Jesus's is not so much a warning as an observation. If you are not involved in justice, by that very fact you are not at the level of sensibility needed to be part of the kingdom. To put it more simply, if you do not stand up for the rights of people, you are not ethically mature enough to consider yourself a follower of Jesus.

7   There is a direct connection between human interaction and religious action. You cannot approach the Divine without being at peace with the human. This is another way of stating the radical nature of the Jesus way: Always seek mutual understanding, rather than putting legal pressure on your fellow human.

8   Here Jesus introduces a psychological dimension into religious questions about moral behavior. As he will say later, moral action comes from who you are and what you think. It is rooted in imagination, and so he wants to address the imagination with stories and with teachings that speak to the heart, not just external behavior. This teaching does not necessarily mean that sexual thoughts and fantasies in general are immoral.

"You're the light of the world. A city on a hill can't be hidden. No one lights a lamp and then shoves it under a pot. You put it on a candle stand to give light to everyone in the house. In the same way, let your light shine on people so they can see your good deeds and honor your father in the sky.[4]

"Don't imagine that I have come to get rid of the law and the prophets. I'm not here to get rid of anything but to complete everything.[5] I'm sincere when I say that until the sky and the earth disappear, not the dot of an 'i' nor a single apostrophe will be lost from the law before everything is accomplished. Anyone who breaks these rules to the slightest degree and tempts others to do so won't have a place in the new era. On the other hand, anyone who keeps and models these rules will be considered great in the new paradigm.

"Be clear about this: Unless your sense of justice is greater than that of the clerks and Pharisees, count on it, you will not enter the kingdom.[6]

"Long ago people were told, 'Don't commit murder. Anyone who does will be damned.' Well, I'm saying that anyone who gets angry with his brother will be damned. Anyone who says to his brother, 'Fool,' is open to the judgment of the court. But anyone who says worse deserves to be hurled into a pit of fire.

"So, if you're placing your offering at the altar and recall that your brother has some grievance against you, set your gift down right there in front of the altar. First make things right with your brother, then, and only then, return to offer your gift.[7]

"Don't hesitate to reach an understanding with your opponent while you're walking down the street with him. Otherwise, he'll hand you over to the judge and the judge will hand you over to a bailiff who will put you in jail. You won't go free until you pay the last penny.

"You've heard it said, 'Don't commit adultery.' But I say that anyone who looks lustfully at a woman[8] has already committed

9 In the kingdom you do not pretend to have God on your side. This may sound surprising, but Jesus recommends asserting your own authority as a person. That is the starting point for your allegiance to the Sky Father and the glorious world he wants to create.

10 These examples show that the values of the kingdom are the opposite of commonly accepted attitudes. Not an eye for an eye, but give more than is asked for. In the Jesus kingdom you always go further in your generosity than is required.

11 A story is told of the famous Zen master Ryokan, who lived in a simple hut at the foot of a mountain. One evening a thief arrived at the hut to find there was nothing to steal. Ryokan said to him, "You have come a long way. Here, take my clothes." The thief was shocked. He took the clothes and went away. Ryokan sat naked, watching the moon. "Poor man," he thought, "I wish I could give him this beautiful moon."

12 In private correspondence with me, Alice O. Howell, an astrologer and Jungian theologian, suggested this translation related to the astrological Uranus. Instead of "sky," "everywhere."

adultery with her in his heart. If your right eye gets you into trouble, pluck it out and toss it away. It's better to lose a single body part than to have your whole body thrown into the pit. If your right hand gets you into trouble, cut it off and toss it away. It's better to lose a single body part than to have your whole body thrown into the pit.[9]

"It's said that anyone who divorces his wife must give her a notice of divorce. But I'm saying that anyone who divorces his wife, except for sexual misconduct, is committing adultery, as is anyone who marries a divorced woman.

"People were once told, 'Don't make an oath if you don't mean it; be sure to honor any oaths you have made to the Lord.' But I'm saying, don't swear at all, whether by the sky, since it's God's throne, or the earth, since it's his footrest, or Jerusalem, since it's the city of the great ruler. And don't swear by your head; I mean, you can't make a hair of it white or black. Just let your words be 'yes' and 'no.' Anything more than this is mistaken. It used to be said, 'An eye for an eye and a tooth for a tooth.' But I'm saying, don't pick a fight with a bad person. If someone slaps you on the right side of the face, turn the other cheek. And if someone wants to hurt you and takes your shirt, give him your coat as well. If someone makes you go one mile with him, go two. If someone wants something from you, give it to him. If someone wants to borrow something, don't turn away.[10]

"You have heard the adage, 'Love your neighbor and hate your enemy.' But I'm telling you, love your enemies and speak well of those who criticize you. This way you can become sons of your father in the sky. For he makes the sun rise on the bad and the good and rain on the just and the unjust. If you love those who love you, what good is that? Anyone can do that. And if you embrace just your brothers, what are you doing that is so special? Doesn't everyone in the world do that? Therefore, be as radically openhearted[11] as your father, who is everywhere."[12]

1   According to this teaching, we should not do good simply to be praised or
    esteemed. It may seem obvious that ego rewards represent a rather low level
    of motivation and yet it is not easy to get free of them. It takes close atten-
    tion, constant awareness, and honest reflection to attain this level of purity
    of intention.

2   "[Eighteenth-century Swedish theologian Emanuel] Swedenborg writes that
    the food and drink that nourish spirits and angels is spiritual and lies in their
    continual desire to know. Spiritual hunger is for knowing, for meaning, and
    knowledge by identity—inner and outer made in a living act of being—is
    daily bread for human beings as spiritual beings."
        —Christopher Bamford, *An Endless Trace: The Passionate Pursuit of Wisdom in the
        West* (New Paltz, NY: Codhill Press, 2003), 43

    Like the religions of India, where *prajna* (knowledge) and *puja* (devotion) are
    linked, Jesus constantly urges deep learning and loving action.

Chapter 6

"When you act compassionately, don't do it in full view so that people can see you. Then you won't have any reward from your father above. When you show compassion, don't toot your own horn, like the hypocrites in the synagogues and on the streets, to get praise from people. They have their reward. No, when you show compassion, don't let your left hand know what your right hand is doing. Be quietly compassionate. Then your father, noticing that you've acted discreetly, will be generous with you.[1]

"When you pray, don't be like hypocrites who like to stand up and pray in the synagogues and the streets so people can see them. They've got what they wanted. When you pray, go into your room, close the door, and pray to your father who can't be seen. Then your father, seeing what is done privately, will reward you. When you pray, don't go on and on like heathens. They think they'll be heard because of the number of words they use. Don't be like them. Your father knows what you want before you ask for it. Pray this way:

Our father in the sky,
May your name be held sacred.
May your kingdom be completed
and your dream fully realized
on earth,
the way it is above.
Provide us with the bread we need today[2]
And forgive anything
we owe you,
just as we forgive anyone
who owes us.

3   *Poneros,* translated here as "losing your soul," is one of several key words in the Gospel. It can mean evil—"deliver us from evil"—but can just as well point to the impact of bad choices—agony, ruin, or self-destruction. In the context of this prayer, *poneros* points to a loss of soul.

4   Forgiveness is one of the pillars of the kingdom. You will be forgiven all of your mistakes in life if you cultivate the spirit of forgiveness in yourself. But forgiveness is not something you can will into existence. It arises when your philosophy of life and moral habits are radically sensitive to others and when you have sorted through a conflict thoroughly. It may take a long while for genuine forgiveness to arise. In the Gospel teaching, *agape* (love), respect, and forgiveness are tightly interconnected.

5   Religious and spiritual people need a heightened level of self-awareness because the inclination to feel superior and to find ego satisfaction in good deeds and deprivations is strong. You have to go through a sometimes painful intellectual and emotional initiation to pull free of the ego and its inclination toward superiority and narcissism.

6   How do you store your valuables in the sky? The sky is an image of spirit. Just as Jesus recommends later that we pay both a Caesar tax and a God tax, here we distinguish between the earthly possessions that we keep in our homes and sky possessions that are our ideals and moral habits, and dreams and visions for a better world. We are beings of earth and sky, not only of the earth.

7   The Gospel way of life requires a sort of stereophonic attention to both spirituality and worldly life. Jesus frequently links ordinary life to spiritual values. Sometimes when people adopt the Gospel teaching, they split life into the religious and the secular. Jesus does not do this. In fact, you might understand him better if you stop thinking of the Gospels as religious teachings and more as a vision for how to be in the world.

Keep us from going wrong,
And save us
from losing our souls.[3]

"If you forgive people when they fail you, your father above will also forgive you. But if you don't forgive people here, your father above won't either.[4]

"When you fast, don't look haggard, as hypocrites do. They make long faces to show that they're hungry. They've received their reward in full. No, when you fast, comb your hair and wash your face, so that people won't even know that you're hungry. Your father alone will know your secret, and quietly he'll reward you.[5]

"Don't pile up earthly possessions. Moths and rust will ruin them and thieves will break in and steal them. Store things that are precious to you in the sky,[6] where moths and rust can't cause damage and where thieves can't break in. Wherever you keep your precious things, that's where your heart will be.

"The eye illuminates the body. If you have good eyes, your body will glow. If your eyes are weak, your body will be dim. If the light in you is actually darkness, that darkness will be intense.

"No one can honor two masters. You'll hate one and love the other or be devoted to one and reject the other. You can't dedicate yourself to both God and godlessness.[7]

8   People often speak of faith as belief in a system or teaching, but Jesus frequently speaks of trust in life. Do not be anxious, he says. Trust that life will
take care of you the way it takes care of flowers. Usually we cannot see our
basic, existential anxiety, our constant worry about survival and thriving.
Jesus teaches profound and radical trust in life as a cure for anxiety.

9   Tradition teaches that Solomon was king of a united Israel. He was the son
of King David and Bathsheba and was known for his wisdom.

10 "Our spiritual being is continually nourished by the countless energies of the
perceptible world."
—Pierre Teilhard de Chardin, *The Divine Milieu* (New York: HarperCollins,
2001), 21

Both Teilhard de Chardin and the Gospel reconnect the spiritual and the
worldly. We need to trust that life sustains at not only the physical level but
also the spiritual level. Jesus consistently lives in and addresses two dimen-
sions: daily life and the realm of the spirit, his friends and his Sky Father. He
says that we have to be sons and daughters of life as well as sons of God.

This beautiful passage about flowers and birds echoes nature metaphors
in other spiritual traditions, such as Taoism and Buddhism. In a famous Zen
story of the "Flower Sermon," the Buddha simply holds up a white flower,
and among his students only Mahakasyapa responds, with a smile, thus
receiving the transmission of the dharma, or the power of the teaching.

"Don't be anxious about life, about what to eat and drink or what clothes to wear. Isn't your soul more important than food[8] and your body more important than clothes? Look at the birds in the sky. They don't plant or harvest or store grain in barns. Your father in the sky feeds them. Aren't you more precious than they are? Can you add a single hour to life by being anxious?

"Why are you so concerned about clothes? Look at the lilies in the field. They don't labor at the spinning wheel. But I'm sure that not even Solomon[9] in all his glory was dressed up like one of them. If that's how God clothes the field with grass that is here today but goes into the fire tomorrow, won't he clothe you even more luxuriously? You need more trust.[10]

"So don't be anxious and whine, 'What will we eat? What will we drink? What will we wear?' Other people worry about these things, but your father above is fully aware of your needs. Before anything else, do what you can to establish his kingdom and sense of compassion, and then these other needs will be taken care of. Don't be anxious about tomorrow. Tomorrow can worry about itself. Every day has enough problems of its own."

1 Remember that the Gospels are not just moral and theological teachings.
They inaugurate a different way for human beings to live on earth. So let
us take this image of the particle and the tree trunk as something more than
moral persuasion and a platitude about judging others. It is a recommenda-
tion for radical self-reflection as a way of life, as opposed to blind, too quick,
and unconscious judging of everything as good or bad. It is about vision,
getting the tree trunk out of your eye, removing any obstacles that may be
preventing you from seeing life with hope and love.

2 Most religions attest to the basic human urge to make petitions from the
source of life. We ask of life the things we need to survive and to thrive. We
ask for ourselves and for one another. To some, petition may appear naive
but it is a fundamental human act. Here, Jesus clearly recommends that we
ask for what we need.

Chapter 7

"**D**on't judge, and you won't be judged. You will be judged the way you judge others. The amount you give is the amount you will receive. Why do you notice the piece of dust in your brother's eye and pay no attention to the tree trunk in your own? How can you say to your brother, 'Let me remove that particle of dust from your eye,' when you have a tree trunk in your own? Don't be a hypocrite. First remove the tree trunk from your eye and then you'll see well enough to take the particle of dust from your brother's eye.[1]

"Don't give sacred objects to dogs and don't cast your pearls before swine. They'll just smash them under their hooves and turn around and maul you. Ask and you'll receive. Look around and you'll discover. Knock and you'll be let in. Everyone who asks will receive, everyone who looks will discover, everyone who knocks will be let in.

"If your child asks for bread, would you hand him a stone? If he asks for a fish, would you give him a snake? You may not be perfect, but you're smart enough to give your children something good, so just imagine the good things that your father above will give to anyone who asks.[2]

"In relation to other people, do for them what you would want them to do for you. This is what the laws and the prophets say.

3   I know the path: it is strait and narrow
     It is like the edge of a sword.
     I rejoice to walk on it
     I weep when I slip.
        —Mahatma Gandhi, in *God Makes the Rivers to Flow: An Anthology of the World's*
        Sacred Poetry and Prose, edited by Eknath Easwaran (Tomales, CA: Nilgiri
        Press, 2003), 202

Here Jesus offers yet another beautiful, basic piece of wisdom: Do not take
the most popular or the easiest path. Your way should be more your own,
maybe more eccentric and individual. Not many, in fact, live by the values
of the kingdom.

     One problem with making the Gospel into a formal religion is that it gets
too big and loses its relevance to the individual person. Jesus's teaching is
subtle and points to a small but crucial shift in the way we look at life. It is
not a social movement but an adjustment to how we see the world.

4   It is one thing to profess an ideal or a value, but something else to act on it.
     Words are not enough.

5   As we have seen again and again, the way of the Sky Father and the new
     kingdom is an alternative to the way we typically live on earth and it turns
     our world inside out. Instead of thinking of ourselves, we think of others.
     Instead of making enemies, we cultivate love and friendship.

6   Make sure that your spiritual life has a solid foundation and on that founda-
     tion cultivate a sense of personal authority. Jesus shows his followers how
     to be like him and share in his authority and power. We are not passive
     followers. In the Gospel teaching we can find our own particular vision
     and direction in life. We do not just follow a teaching; we develop our
     own values and way of life that we defend courageously, inspired by the
     strength with which Jesus presented his philosophy against strong criticism
     and threat of persecution. The Gospel is our model, not our rulebook.

"Go through the narrow gate, because the wide gate and the broad road lead to disaster. Many go that way, of course, and yet a narrow gate and a little lane lead to life. Unfortunately, few choose them.[3]

"Watch out for pseudo-prophets. They come to you dressed up like sheep, but inside they're hungry wolves. You'll recognize them by their fruits. Do people pick grapes from thornbushes and figs from thistles? It's the same with trees: Good ones have good fruit and bad ones, bad. A good tree won't grow bad fruit and a bad tree won't grow good fruit. Furthermore, any tree that doesn't grow good fruit gets cut down and goes into the fire. No doubt about it—you'll recognize them by their fruit.[4]

"Not everyone who says to me, 'Master, Master,' will enter the kingdom, but only those who follow the way of the father above.[5] On the crucial day many will say to me, 'Master, Master, we stood up for your name, didn't we? Didn't we rid ourselves of our demonic tendencies and demonstrate incredible powers?' Then I will tell them, 'I don't know you. Get away from me. You don't belong here.'

"Anyone who hears my words and puts them into practice is like a thoughtful person who built his house on rock. The rains came and the streams rose and the winds blew and smashed against that house. But did it collapse? No, because its foundation was rock. Anyone who hears my words and doesn't act on them is like a thoughtless man who built his house on sand. The rains came and the streams rose and the winds blew and smashed against his house and it collapsed with a huge crash."[6]

When Jesus finished speaking, the crowd sat stunned. He taught like someone with authority and not like the legalists they were used to.

1   This passage contrasts the lack of trust in the chosen people, those you think would be full of trust, and the Roman occupier who might be considered an infidel. The Roman soldier has the greatest faith.

2   This is a constant theme. The people who should understand and accept the Jesus kingdom reject it, but those who seem to have no background for it and are the least likely to "get" it, like the centurion, respond positively. Imagine praising a soldier who is occupying your country for his wisdom and character. The foreigner has it right. Or today it might be the atheist or the one who does not go to church or who does not pray in the usual way. You cannot decide if the Jesus kingdom is in play through surface signs, like formal rituals and pious language. You have to look past the obvious and the stereotypical. In public life we still measure a nation's degree of spirituality by counting the number of people going to church, rather than using a qualitative measure of values and vision.

Chapter 8

When Jesus came down from the mountain, a large crowd gathered around him. A man with skin lesions came along and bowed and said, "Sir, if you wanted to, you could take away my illness."

He reached out and touched the man. "I'm happy to do this," he said. "Clear up." Immediately his skin lesions went away. Jesus said to him, "Be careful not to tell anyone. But go and show yourself to the priest and offer the gift that Moses prescribed in thanks for your healing."

After Jesus arrived at Capernaum, a centurion approached him and asked for help. "Sir," he said, "my servant is at home. He's paralyzed and suffering terribly."

Jesus said, "I'll go and attend to him."

The centurion responded, "Sir, I'm not worthy to have you under my roof. Just say a word and he'll get better. I'm someone who knows what it's like to be under authority. I have soldiers under me. If I say to one of them, 'Go,' he goes. To another, 'Come,' he comes. If I tell my servant, 'Do this,' he does it."

Jesus heard this and was impressed and told those around him, "I have to say, I have never come across anyone in Israel with such trust.[1] Many will come from East and West and share the kingdom with Abraham, Isaac, and Jacob. But those who would seem to be citizens of the kingdom will be tossed outside, where they will weep and grit their teeth."[2]

Then Jesus told the centurion, "Go on, now. It will all turn out as you hope it will." The centarion's servant got better that very hour.

3   Isaiah 53:4.

4   In Robert W. Funk's superb short book *Jesus as Precursor*, there is a chapter titled "Jesus as Saunterer" that effectively compares the thoughts and styles of Henry David Thoreau and Jesus. For example, Funk says, "The locus of the sacred had shifted for [Jesus] from the temple to the marketplace, from the synagogue to the crossroads" (Funk).

In *Conjectures of a Guilty Bystander*, Thomas Merton observes, "Thoreau's idleness (as 'inspector of snowstorms,' Walden) was an incomparable gift and its fruits were blessings that America has never really learned to appreciate" (Merton).

This shift from the temple to the marketplace could finally free the Gospel from its imprisonment in rigid religious practice. It is a simple and subtle change, but it is essential and speaks to the core of the Gospel teaching.

5   This order is perhaps too strong when taken only literally. First, there will always be an excuse not to enter the kingdom and live at a higher and deeper level. Second, Jesus is all about life, not death. Consider this in light of Freud's "death principle," sometimes called *thanatos*, after the Greek word for death. Your spirit can die off in legalism and moralism or it can come to life in the compassion-based philosophy of the kingdom. The *thanatos* institutions get it wrong; the people who opt for life are following the Gospel.

When Jesus arrived at Peter's house, he saw Peter's mother-in-law in bed with a fever. He touched her hand and the fever went away. She got up then and tended him.

When it was evening, they brought several daimonically disturbed people to him, and he got rid of the spirits with a word and took care of all the sick. This fulfilled the saying of the prophet Isaiah:

> *He carried our sicknesses*
> *and bore our illnesses.*[3]

When Jesus saw the crowd around him, he gave the order to go across to the other side of the lake. There a law professor came along and said, "Teacher, I will follow you wherever you go." Jesus replied, "Foxes have holes and birds of the sky have nests, but this human being has nowhere to lay his head."[4]

One of his followers said, "First let me go to my father's funeral."

Jesus said to him, "Follow me and let the dead bury their own dead."[5]

He got into a boat and his followers joined him. All of a sudden, a strong storm whipped up on the lake. Water splashed over the boat. But he went on sleeping. Finally, they woke him up and said, "Sir, save us. We're going to die."

He said to them, "Where's your trust? Why are you afraid?"

Then he got up and commanded the winds and the sea and it became completely calm. They were stunned and wondered, "What kind of person is this? The winds and the seas do what he says."

6   "Pork becomes unclean and pigs become 'disgusting' when the mother func-
    tions of the feminine, and the goddess of rotting and rutting and spring-to-
    life, are no longer revered."
        —Nor Hall, *The Moon and the Virgin: Reflections on the Archetypal Feminine* (New
        York: Harper & Row, 1980), 81–82

Nor Hall, a depth psychologist who writes about feminine mysteries, points
out that the ancient Greeks told a story about Iambe, a servant of the great
goddess Demeter, whose husband tended a herd of pigs that fell into a
chasm. Jesus listens to the powers that have possessed the insane men and
understands that they are related to the pigs. His "exorcism" brings them
back to their proper place.

    The demons usually claim a connection with Jesus, even familiarity, and
here they ask to return to their natural pig bodies. Jesus takes them out of the
neurotic human context and returns them to where they more naturally have
a home. Their dying in the water is like returning to their source. When we
deny our basic piglike passions, we may become hysterical; we are overtaken
by strong feelings that need a place in our approach to life. Jesus heals by
paying attention to the spirit that has overtaken the men and responding to
their needs.

When he landed on the other side, in the area of Gadarenes, two possessed men coming from the graveyard met up with him. They were so disturbed that no one dared go into that area.

"What do you want from us? Have you come to torment us now?"

A large herd of pigs was a ways off, grazing. The spirits begged him, "If you're going to force us out, drive us into those pigs gathered over there." He said to them, "Go," and they went out into the pigs, and the whole herd sped down the steep bank into the lake and died in the water.[6] The herdsmen ran away and went into town and told the whole story, including what had happened to the disturbed people. Then the whole town went out to meet Jesus, and when they saw him asked him to leave their area.

1   His town was Capernaum, the center of his activities. He taught in the syna-
    gogue there.

2   Often called "scribes," these were "qualified jurists, who gathered round
    themselves circles of disciples. It was they, residing mostly at Jerusalem,
    who decided what details of conduct were required in order to give practical
    effect to the Law" (Grant).

3   "He profess'd that he came not to call the Righteous but Sinners to Repen-
    tance; which imply'd his modest Opinion that there were some in his Time
    so good that they need not hear even for Improvement; but now a days we
    have scarce a little Parson, that does not think it the Duty of every Man
    within his Reach to sit under his petty Ministrations, and that whoever omits
    them offends God."
        —Benjamin Franklin, "Letter to Joseph Huey, June 6, 1753," in *Letters of a
        Nation: A Collection of Extraordinary American Letters*, edited by Andrew Carroll
        (New York: Kodansha International, 1997), 392

    Benjamin Franklin offers one reason why Jesus associates with shady charac-
    ters, but another is that he simply is not a religious purist. He loves life, and
    his teaching is about living well and lovingly. He is not a moralist, dividing
    the world into the good and the bad. He appreciates people who dare to
    live, rather than shrouding themselves in virtue, even if they make mistakes.

Chapter 9

J esus got in a boat and crossed the lake and went to his own
town.¹ There he ran into some people carrying a man who
was paralyzed and lying on a cot. When Jesus saw how trusting
they were, he said to the man, "Stop carrying this burden of
yours. Your guilt is gone. You're clean."

Some of the law experts² grumbled, "This man is being
sacrilegious."

But Jesus, aware of their thoughts, said, "Is it easier to say,
'Get up and walk' or 'Your guilt is gone'?" But so you understand
that the son of man has the authority to forgive human errors,
he said to the sick man, "Get up, take your cot, and go home."
When the crowd saw all this, they were awestruck and praised
God for giving human beings such authority.

As Jesus was walking along, he noticed a man named Matthew
sitting at the revenue officer's stand. "Join me," he told him.
Matthew got up and followed him.

Jesus had dinner at Matthew's house, and several tax collectors and unsavory people came and ate with him and his followers. When the Pharisees saw all this, they asked his students,
"Why does your teacher dine with tax collectors and disreputable people?"

Jesus overheard them and said, "Healthy people don't need
a doctor, but the sick do.³ Remember the saying: 'I want mercy,
not sacrifice.' I haven't come to win over those who always live
properly, but those who have made serious mistakes."

4 Among other things, this remark suggests that Jesus's way should be joyful, not somber. The time to be depressed is when you are struggling without the benefit of his inspiring vision. Being outside the kingdom is depressing. Or, maybe nonclinical depression could be defined as living without a positive philosophy and a loving heart.

5 The externals of the spiritual life quickly become old and rigid, and so they need to be renewed regularly. The archetype of the reformer is as important as that of the follower and apostle.

6 Once again it would be helpful to switch from faith to trust. Rather than focusing on believing in intellectual truths, we might develop more trust in life. Trust in an opening of the heart, letting life flow through us, rather than binding our minds to a particular system of thought.

7 In this section we come across one of the key Gospel terms: *egersis*, getting up after lying down. The man gets up from his cot and the girl gets up from her sleep. Later we will see that Jesus gets up from death—often translated as "risen from the dead." We can get up from our sleep, our unconsciousness, and in that sense be resurrected people, filled with new life. The Gospels encourage us to get up off our cots and up from our sleep. The word is also used for erecting a building—we have a kingdom to make. The word is equal in importance to *metanoia* and *agape*.

Then John's followers approached and asked him, "How do you explain the fact that we and the Pharisees fast, but your followers don't?"

Jesus replied, "Why would the groom's guests not eat while he is with them? Eventually, the groom will go away.[4] Then they can fast. No one sews a patch of unwashed fabric onto a garment. The patch won't hold and it will make the tear worse. People don't put fresh wine in old leather winebags. If they do that, the bags will burst, the wine will leak out, and the bags will be ruined. Instead, they pour fresh wine into new bags and then everything is fine."[5]

As he was speaking, a politician approached and knelt in front of him and sobbed, "My daughter died a while ago. If you just put your hand on her, she'll be OK. She'll live." Jesus got up and accompanied him. The students went along as well.

But then a woman who for twelve years had suffered from internal bleeding came up behind him and touched the edge of his coat. She said to herself, "If I just brush against his coat, I'll be healed."

Jesus turned around and looked at her. "Have courage, young woman. Your trust has healed you." At that very moment the woman got better.[6]

Finally, when Jesus entered the house of the politician and saw the flute players and a rowdy crowd, he said, "Go away. The girl isn't dead. She's sleeping." They laughed at him. But when the crowd had been ushered out, he went in and took the girl by the hand and she got up.[7] News of this event spread throughout the region.

8   The people often sense that Jesus is somehow in tune with the dark spirits, perhaps with spirits in general. He understands them, and they know him. Jesus and the spirits can speak to each other. Many times Jesus looks like a shaman, one who knows the upper worlds and the lower ones.

9   The situation is the same today. The physical, emotional, and spiritual needs of the world are great. We need good, solid, visionary ideas, and leadership that is based on service rather than ideology and ego. Jesus models this leadership and also models how to train leaders. He gives his students and followers instructions on how to be teachers and healers.

Jesus went on from there and two blind men near him cried out, "Help us kindly, son of David."

When he was indoors, the blind men approached him and he asked them, "Are you sure that I can help you?"

"Yes, sir," they answered.

He touched their eyes and said, "Because of your trust, let it happen." Their sight came back to them and Jesus warned them sternly, "Be sure that no one finds out about this." But they went out and told the story everywhere they went.

As they exited, a man possessed by a daimonic force and unable to speak came to Jesus. Afterward, when the daimonic element had been expelled, the man started talking. The people in the vicinity were stunned. "We've never seen anything like this in Israel."

But the Pharisees complained, "It is by the leader of the demonic, the prince of the demons, that he could exorcise this thing."[8]

Jesus traveled through all the cities and towns, teaching in the synagogues, spreading the welcome news about the kingdom, and caring for people with all kinds of illness and disease. When he beheld the masses of people, he felt compassionate because they were being prodded and provoked. They were like sheep without a shepherd. He told his followers, "The harvest is abundant but the workers are few. Ask the harvest master to send workers into his field."[9]

1 Jesus transmits his power to heal and to teach to his select students. The Greek word is usually *mathetes*, "student," rather than *apostolos*, "apostle," which means someone who is sent. The first step is to be a good student— learn the Jesus way. Develop an intelligence about life based on his teaching. Eventually, this learning transforms you into a person with the power to deal with compulsions, moralism, and rigid dogmatism. You become egoless and a lover of people and of life, as Jesus was.

2 Again, the word is *egeirete*, the same word for those who "get up" after being laid low by sickness and for Jesus after he "got up" from the dead (Matthew 27:53).

3 This paragraph may be the best summary of how to live kingdom values: care for the sick, wake up the unconscious, bring relief (catharsis) to those who are suffering and rejected, and get rid of the demonic. All of these together point to the prime value: respect all beings, especially those not in your circle.

Chapter 10

He gathered his twelve students together and gave them authority over spirits and the power to deal with every illness and disease.[1]

These are the names of his twelve students: first, Simon, called Peter, and his brother Andrew; James, the son of Zebedee, and his brother John; Philip and Bartholomew; Thomas and Matthew the tax collector; James, the son of Alphaeus; Theaddaeus; Simon the Zealot; and Judas Iscariot, who betrayed him.

Jesus commissioned these twelve: "Don't go just anywhere. Don't enter a town of Samaritans. Instead, go to the lost sheep of the house of Israel. When you're out there, emphasize these themes:

> *The kingdom is drawing near.*
> *Care for those who are suffering.*
> *Wake up*[2] *those who are unconscious.*
> *Refresh those who have suffered.*
> *Get rid of daimonic tendencies.*[3]

"You have received a great deal without having to pay for it; now give back without charging anything. Don't put any gold, copper, or silver in your wallets. Don't take any luggage for the journey. No extra garment or sandals or even a walking stick.

"A worker is worth his care. Whenever you come into a town or village, find a good person there and stay with him until you leave. When you enter a home, offer a friendly greeting. If the home is a good one, fill it with your peace. If it's bad, keep your peace to yourself. If people won't welcome you or listen to your words, shake the dust off your feet when you leave that house

4   This reference to morally corrupt towns does not have to be seen as a damn-
    ing as much as a statement of fact. Any community that does not live by the
    Gospel teaching of love, going beyond moralism and legalism, is doomed to
    suffer by virtue of who they are. In other words, if our world could live from
    a more open heart, many of our problems would be solved.

5   Sometimes the Gospel teaching is presented as all dove and no snake. This
    combination suggests a more complex view of Jesus than the usual one.

6   Jesus understands, as all prophets come to grasp, that visionary ideas are a
    threat to the status quo. People's fear turns into annoyance and aggression,
    and the lives of our greatest prophets end violently.

7   Although Jesus teaches a philosophy of love, his is a tough love. He does
    not seem to have much patience with rigidity and intransigence. If they do
    not listen to you, move on, he says. The passage also gives a strong hint that
    Jesus intends his teachings for the whole world, not just for people who sign
    up with him.

8   Again, Jesus makes it clear that he is concerned about the soul, not just
    physical life. For all his healings and social ideas, his teachings address the
    interior life as well.

9   Gehenna—this vale of tears, this realm of *samsara*, this cruel world.

or town. I assure you, it would be easier for Sodom and Gomorrah on the day when they are judged than for that town.[4]

"I am sending you out like sheep among wolves. So be as sharp-witted as snakes and as innocent as doves.[5] Be cautious around people. They will report you to local authorities and beat you in their synagogues. When they arrest you, don't worry about what to say or how to say it. At the right time you will be given the words you need. Anyway, it won't be you speaking but the spirit of the father speaking in you.

"Brother will betray brother and a father his child—to death. Children will turn against their parents and have them put to death.[6] Because they will associate you with my name, everyone will hate you. But whoever remains steadfast will be spared.

"When they give you trouble in one town, go on to the next one. I assure you, you won't make it through all the cities of Israel before the son of man comes.[7]

"A follower is not above his teacher or a servant above his master. It's proper for a follower be like his teacher and the servant his master. If they call the master of the house Beelzeboul, what are they going to call members of the household?

"So don't be afraid of them. Nothing is covered up that won't be uncovered, nothing hidden that won't be revealed. What I tell you in darkness, say in the daylight. What you hear softly with your ears, proclaim from the rooftops. Don't be afraid of anyone who can kill the body but not the soul.[8] Rather, be afraid of anyone in this valley of Gehenna[9] who can destroy both soul and body.

10 From a spiritual point of view, every person is of the greatest importance. Psychologically, you should know of your immeasurable value as a person. And you might have the same feeling about everyone else, especially those who superficially appear to be worthless. This is another area when the view from the kingdom differs from the usual set of values. We see through superficial matters of economic status and educational level to the worth of the person.

11 In this context, Jesus admits that his teaching may be divisive and challenging. He is not innocent about his mission. When taken seriously, it could completely disrupt the way we do things in our personal lives and in society. As always, change for the better means an end to the status quo.

12 Micah 7:6. Here and in other passages Jesus makes it clear that our real friends are not necessarily those of our own nationality, belief system, or even family. The values of the kingdom create new and deeper ties among people. People who live the Jesus values gravitate toward each other and form new "family" ties and new communal relationships. This does not necessarily mean church affiliations but worldwide communities of people who want a loving world.

13 This is often translated to imply love, but the Greek word, *philia*, suggests friendship. Friendship is a key form of love in the kingdom. You see it exemplified in Jesus's love for his friends, the men and women around him especially. He models friendship as a major way of creating community.

14 This statement may sound harsh. Perhaps it refers to the kingdom as a higher or more intense kind of life, where you do not leave behind feelings for family but transcend them for the greater good, for the world community. Especially when you have a conflict between family concerns and the good of the world, you should at least consider the importance of the larger community. Most socially minded people face this conflict at one time or another.

"You know, of course, that two sparrows are worth about a penny? And yet not even one of them falls to the ground without your father's knowledge. Every hair of your head is accounted for. So don't worry. You are worth more than many sparrows.[10]

"Anyone who speaks in my favor in public I will speak in favor of before my father above. But anyone who disowns me in public, I will disown to my father above. Don't assume that I have come to bring peace on earth. I didn't come to bring peace, but a sword.[11]

> *I have come to turn*
> *A man against his father,*
> *A daughter against her mother, and*
> *A daughter-in-law against her mother-in-law.*
> *A person's enemies will be the members of*
> *His own household.*[12]

"Anyone who is closer[13] to his father or mother than to me is not worthy of me. Anyone who loves his son or daughter more than me is not worthy of me.[14]

15 This is one of those paradoxical statements that often appear in the Gospels. If you feel that you possess your soul and understand your world and do not change, eventually you will become lost. But if you lose the life that you have known and adopt the radical new vision of the Gospels, you will keep your soul and make discoveries about it that you would never have expected.

16 If you live by the law of love presented in the Gospels, you will be in harmony with the Sky Father and the deep law of the universe. This choice puts you in tune with the deepest way, or Tao, the divine course at the heart of existence. Jesus's constant reference to the Father takes his message out of a purely personal context, connecting your personal way of life with the core rules of existence. You are in tune with the secret ways of the cosmos.

"Anyone who finds his soul will lose it. Anyone who loses his soul for my sake will find it.[15]

"Whoever takes you in takes me in, and whoever takes me in takes in the one who sent me.[16] If anyone takes in a prophet because he is a prophet, he will have a prophet's reward, and anyone who takes in an honorable man because he is honorable will have an appropriate reward. If anyone gives so much as a cup of cold water to one of these little ones as my follower, he will certainly have his reward."

1   Malachi 3:1.

2   If you are living the values of the kingdom—love, compassion, forgiveness, conviviality, healing, dealing with demonic factors in your heart, extending your concern beyond your own circle—then you are a complete person. Even the greatest spiritual masters are not above you. Although humility has its place, it is also important to have a solid sense of your infinite value. I might push this idea further: If you embody the Gospel kingdom in your life and person, you are an equal to Jesus. As the remarkable Renaissance Christian theologian Nicolas of Cusa said, "You are a divine human."

Incidentally, John is a precursor of Jesus in the sense that he lived and promoted the basics of the Gospel before Jesus arrived with the full message.

3   History shows that whenever someone appears doing good and living by a set of values more compassionate and egalitarian than the usual, this person is often persecuted, if not killed. In fact, this is an aspect of the Jesus archetype—the visionary whose life is cut short. We might all remember this full picture of the Jesus way when people criticize us or give us trouble because of our values.

Chapter 11

After Jesus had finished instructing his twelve students, he went on to teach and speak in the towns of Galilee. When John in prison heard about the activities of Christos, the anointed man, he sent his followers to ask him, "Are you the one we are waiting for or should we expect someone else?"

Jesus answered, "Go back and tell John what you've heard and seen: The blind see, the crippled walk, the sick get better, the deaf hear, the unconscious ones wake up, and the poor are given a hopeful message. Anyone who isn't shocked by me is in a state of bliss."

As John's followers were leaving, Jesus said of John, "What did you go out into the desert to see? A reed undulating in the wind? No? A man dressed up in elegant attire? No. Those dressed in fine clothes are in the palaces of kings. Well, what did you go to see? A prophet? Yes, and more than a prophet. This is the man about whom it is written:

> *I will send my messenger ahead of you*
> *To prepare your path.* [1]

"I can tell you that there isn't a human being greater than John the Baptist. Yet, the very least among those in the kingdom is greater than he is. [2] Since the time of John the Baptist right up until now, violent people have attacked the kingdom, but it has always been strong. [3]

"The teaching of the prophets and the law and of course John have looked forward to this event, and perhaps you are willing to accept it: The one everyone is waiting for is Elijah.

4 This is an important point for people looking to live out a Gospel-based spirituality. It is not ascetic. Although it is tempting to assume that being spiritual means denying yourself earthly pleasures, Jesus affirms the ordinary joys of life. Of course, those who confused self-denial with real virtue criticized Jesus for his apparent worldliness.

5 This day of judgment can be any day on which who we are and what we have done is revealed and evaluated. Have we contributed or stood in the way? Have we chosen to live with an open heart? Have we dealt with our rage and other difficult passions? What kind of people are we? This judgment can happen in our own thoughts or in the way the world regards us. In other words, the day of judgment is any and every day, as we evaluate our lives.

"Can you hear me? Listen.

"What can I compare this generation to? They are like children at the market shouting to one another:

> *We played the flute for you*
> *And you didn't dance.*
> *We wept and you didn't mourn.*

"John didn't eat or drink much and they said, 'He's possessed.' The son of man arrived and ate and drank⁴ and they said, 'Look, a glutton and a drunkard, a friend of tax collectors and riffraff.'

"You teach wisdom by what you do."

Then he began to criticize the cities in which he had shown his powers because they didn't change their ways. "Shame on you, Chorazin. Shame on you, Bethsaida. If the displays of power you have witnessed had been done in Tyre and Sidon, they would have shown their change of heart by wearing coarse cloth and placing ash on their heads. I'm telling you that on the day they face judgment they'd be better off being Tyre and Sidon. What about you, Capernaum? Will you ascend into the sky? No, you'll be lowered into Hades. If the wonders done for you had taken place in Sodom, it would be standing today. I can tell you this: On the day of judgment it will be easier for Sodom than for you."⁵

At that moment Jesus said, "I praise you, Father, Lord of earth and sky, because you have hidden these things from the wise and learned and revealed them to toddlers. Yes, Father, this is what you so graciously wanted.

6 This idea comes through again and again: Jesus reveals the Father's will and plan. You can understand "father" as the inner law or source of life. To know the Father's plan through the teachings of Jesus is to have insight into the very nature of reality. Follow the teaching and you are in accord with the deep cosmic laws. In this, the Jesus way is akin to the Tao in Chinese spiritual thought or dharma in Buddhism. In our time we tend to emphasize the personal dimension, but our lives would deepen and broaden if we imagined ourselves being attuned to the laws that govern the natural world.

"My father put everything in my hands. No one recognizes the son except the father, and no one recognizes the father except the son and anyone to whom the son wants to reveal him.[6]

"Come to me all of you who are tired and oppressed. I'll refresh you. Rest your weight on my shoulders and learn from me, because I am gentle and humble at heart. In me you'll find rest for your souls. The demands I put on your back are not all that difficult. In fact, the load is light."

1   Jesus's teaching here sounds radical even today. Following his teaching, you
    may break certain rules, especially the very formal ones you grew up with.
    He is not concerned about the letter of the law. If you live by his rule of
    love, you may break conventional rules, and be criticized and even punished
    for it. But you will be serving a higher purpose. Here is another way of say-
    ing this: Living by the vital pulse of love often entails some degree of trans-
    gression. You will always be offending someone and may well be a challenge
    to those around you who prefer a more stable and conventional philosophy.
    Jesus is a radical utopian.

2   History reveals this pattern again and again: Someone stands up for simple
    humane values and the authorities plot to get rid of him or her, contradicting
    their own ideals of justice and a good society. This unfortunate pattern is
    part of the Jesus archetype, a fate that has befallen many good people.

Chapter 12

It was the Sabbath and Jesus was walking through fields of grain. His followers were hungry and began to pick ears of corn and munch on them. When the Pharisees saw this, they said to him, "What your followers are doing is not allowed on the Sabbath."

He said, "Have you ever read about what David did when he and his companions were hungry? He went into the house of God and he and his friends ate the sacred bread. It was not legal for them to do this, because only the priests were allowed. Have you ever read in the Book of Laws that the priests in the temple break the Sabbath and yet they haven't done anything wrong? I'm telling you, what you see here is something greater than the temple. If you understood these words, 'I want tender hearts, not self-sacrifice,' you wouldn't have judged these people who are guilty of nothing. The son of man is master of the Sabbath."[1]

He left there and went to their synagogue and a man with a shrunken hand was present. Thinking they could condemn Jesus, the Pharisees asked him, "Is it legal to heal on the Sabbath?"

He replied, "Say one of you has a sheep that falls into a hole on the Sabbath. Wouldn't you grab it and pull it out? Yet a man is much more precious than a sheep. Yes, it is legal to do something good on the Sabbath."

Then he addressed the man, "Put out your hand." He put his hand out and it was like new and as healthy as the other one. But the Pharisees went off and plotted how they might kill Jesus.[2] Alerted to the plot, Jesus left there.

3   Isaiah 42:1–4.

4   A pagan divinity, "Lord of the Temple," or the prince of dung or flies, a name for the absolute demonic.

5   Here, for the first time, we come upon "the kingdom of God." We could imagine this "kingdom" as the world of meaning created by the new way that Jesus is spelling out, step-by-step, a new vision of how human life can be. This divine kingdom is a new world, a new era, a way of life based on principles entirely different from the normally accepted ones.

Dealing effectively with the demonic forces that afflict the world would be a sign that the new kingdom has arrived. The "demonic" might include narcissism, greed, aggression, jealousy, competition, or violence. Existential psychologist Rollo May defines the "daimonic" as "any natural function which has the power to take over the whole person. Sex and eros, anger and rage, and the craving for power are examples. The daimonic can be either creative or destructive and is normally both. When this power goes awry, and one element usurps control over the total personality, we have 'daimon possession,' the traditional name through history for psychosis" (May).

Most of us know in ourselves or others what it is like to feel possessed. Momentarily we are not present, but something has taken over us.

Many people followed him and he tended all the sick among them and told them not to talk about him. This fulfilled what the prophet Isaiah said:

> *This is my child and I have chosen him.*
> *I love him and enjoy him.*
> *I will place my spirit upon him*
> *And he will teach compassion to all people.*
> *He will not be divisive or strident.*
> *No one will hear his voice in the streets.*
> *He won't break a rotting reed*
> *Or snuff out a smoldering wick.*
> *As he is creating a compassionate world,*
> *People everywhere will put their hope*
> *In his name.*[3]

Then they brought him a man daimonically possessed who was blind and mute, and he healed him. Now the man could speak and see. The people were amazed and said, "Can this one be the son of David?" But when the Pharisees heard this, they said, "It is by Beelzeboul, the prince of the demons, that this man expels demons."

Aware of their negative attitude, Jesus said to them, "Every kingdom that is polarized is set up for ruin. No city or house divided against itself can stand. If Satan tries to do away with Satan, he is himself polarized. How can his kingdom survive? If I expel demons by Beelzeboul,[4] the prince of demons, the Lord of the Flies, how do you get rid of them? You must do it the same way.

"But if I expel the daimonic through the spirit of God, you will be able to see the kingdom of God.[5]

6 The context here is exorcism, which we might reconsider for our time. It means to liberate a person or a group from the negative passion that dominates and controls them. Some people need to be freed from their racism or deep anger. In Jesus's depth psychology, you have to bind this strong influence before you can eradicate its power. You cannot be free of it unless first you use your own strength to keep it from having such an influence. Then you can root it out.

7 You do not have to be an explicit follower of Jesus, but if you are not shaped by the spirit of holiness and a sense of the sacred you are indeed lost. The kingdom is not a formal religion but it does aim for holiness and spiritual depth.

8 You do not have to think of the "day of judgment" as some apocalyptic day in the future. Any moment you feel compelled to assess your life, perhaps due to some overwhelming misfortune, you may discover that you are who you are because of choices you have made.

9 Here Jesus compares his life to the image of Jonah and the pattern of death and resurrection. Throughout history, theologians have compared Jesus to Adonis, Dionysus, and other gods of dying and resurrecting. In his image, any of us may die to an old self and rise into a new way of life and a new personality. If you want to follow the Gospel way, you might take this pattern seriously. You may frequently experience a dying of the self and a rising into a new vision and new vitality.

"How can anyone enter the strong man's house and run off with his things, unless first he ties him up? Then he can ravage the house.[6]

"If you're not with me, you're against me. If you don't join me, you fall apart. You lose your center. As I see it, every wrong act and blasphemy can be forgiven, except blasphemy against the spirit, which can't be forgiven. If someone speaks against the son of man, he'll be forgiven. But if he speaks against the holy spirit, he won't be forgiven, not now or in the future.[7]

"Grow a good tree, and its fruit will be good. Grow an inferior tree, and its fruit will be bad. You can gauge a tree by its fruit.

"You brood of vipers. Your ways are corrupt, so how can you say anything good? Your mouth utters whatever fills your hearts. The good person engages in good behavior from the good he has stored up in him. The bad person engages in destructive behavior from the bad he has stored up in him. The day they face judgment,[8] people will have to account for every thoughtless word they've uttered. Your words will make you either innocent or guilty."

Then a few lawyers and Pharisees said to him, "We want to see some sign or omen about you."

His reply: "A wicked, godless people asks for an omen. The only omen you'll get is the image of the prophet Jonah. Just as Jonah spent three days and nights in the belly of the fish, so the son of man will spend three days and nights in the heart of the earth.[9]

10 The Greek word here is a form of *metanoia*, not "repentance" but "change."

"Repentance is not a free and fair highway to God. A wise man will dispense with repentance.... God prefers that you approach him thoughtful, not penitent, though you are the chief of sinners. It is only by forgetting yourself that you draw near to him."
—Henry David Thoreau, *I to Myself*, edited by Jeffrey S. Cramer (New Haven, CT: Yale University Press, 2007), 47

The deep change in your attitude toward the world, especially from ego-centeredness to openhearted concern, is perhaps the first basic step in the Jesus way.

11 The Queen of Sheba, perhaps present-day Yemen, came from a great distance to meet Solomon and test his wisdom. Here Jesus says that in his teaching she would find a greater wisdom. Artists have often painted this captivating story and portrayed its many different interpretations. The most timely for today sees her as Solomon's equal, whose visit was to her advantage.

12 Repeatedly, Jesus raises the level of whatever is under consideration through parable or some other literary image. He is ever the poet, moving away from literal and pragmatic expressions to matters that are more refined and ultimately more significant. His words here about his mother and family will seem harsh only if taken literally. He is simply saying that a new human family can come into existence for those who adopt his way of thinking. The sense of family expands and becomes less literal.

"The men of Nineveh will stand up to judge this lot and condemn them. When Jonah spoke, they changed their ways.[10] But now, here is someone greater than Jonah. The Queen of the South,[11] too, will stand up to judge this group and condemn them. She traveled from the ends of the earth to hear Solomon's wisdom. But now here is someone greater than Solomon.

"When an unclean spirit comes out of a person, it looks for a place in the desert to rest and doesn't find it. Then it thinks, 'I'll go back to the home I had.' When it gets there, it finds the home cleaned up and put in order. Then it goes on and finds seven spirits even more wicked, and they go in and live there. And so that person is worse now than he was before. This is the way it will be with the wicked."

While Jesus was speaking to the crowd, his mother and brothers were standing off to the side, wanting to talk to him. Someone told him and he said, "Who is my mother and who are my brothers?" He gestured toward his followers and said, "Here are my mother and my brothers. Whoever does what my father above wishes them to do is my mother and sister and brother."[12]

1   "[People] are sown on earth as material for the Kingdom of Heaven—some by the wayside, some on rocky ground, some among thorns and some on good soil. It is only those in the last class that are capable of understanding that inner evolution that brings them to the level of the Kingdom."
    —Maurice Nicoll, *The New Man* (New York: Penguin Books, 1967), 159

Nicoll offers another good translation of the key word *metanoia*: "inner evolution."

2   The Greek word here is *mysteria*, "mysteries." If you are a follower of Jesus's teachings, you are in touch with the mysteries of the sky/spiritual kingdom. Here we have an explicit reference to the teachings as mysteries, a key word in the spiritual life. If we do not appreciate the place of the mysterious, we spend our time trying to explain everything, rather than reflecting, praying, and using ritual. There are methods to connect with mysteries and other methods to dispel them.

    What if we saw Jesus himself as a mystery? Or his birth, his healings, and his resurrection not as facts, but as mysteries to ponder without complete explanation?

3   You have to come to the idea of the kingdom with some willingness, trust, appreciation, and lack of prejudice. The religious authorities of Jesus's time came full of rules and expectations. These would be taken away from them. If they have no openness to the Jesus message, that closed-mindedness, too, will do them in. If you do not have even enough character to take an interest in this kingdom, you will be left out in the cold. Parable after parable makes this point.

4   This is not the only time Jesus says that he speaks in parables, a shocking story that turns ordinary ways of thinking upside down. It is as if Jesus were saying: Some things can only be described in stories that make you think, stories that may turn your world around. You need to be shocked into awareness, because my teaching cannot be explained step-by-step or rationally.

Chapter 13

That same day Jesus went out and sat by the water and a large crowd gathered around him. He got into a boat and sat down, while the people remained standing on the shore, and he spoke to them mainly in parables.

For example: "A sower went out and sowed some seed. As he was tossing the seeds, some fell on the road and birds came and ate them. Some fell on stony areas where there wasn't much soil. They sprouted quickly because the soil was shallow. But then when the sun rose they dried up and withered because they didn't have roots. Other seeds fell among brambles that grew and choked the plants. Other seeds fell on good soil and produced a good crop, as much as a hundred, sixty, or thirty times the seeds planted. Try to understand this."[1]

His followers approached him and asked, "Why do you speak in parables?"

He answered, "You have the privilege of knowing the mysteries[2] of the kingdom, but they don't. If you have something already, you will be given more and have a lot. But if you don't have anything, what you have will be taken away.[3] I speak to them in parables because they see and yet don't see.[4] They hear and yet don't hear. And they certainly don't understand. They fulfill the prophecy of Isaiah:

> *You will always hear but not understand.*
> *You will always see but not really perceive.*

5   Isaiah 6:9–10.

6   "When Hindus go to a temple, they do not commonly say, 'I am going to worship,' but rather, 'I am going for *darsan*.' They go to 'see' the image of the deity.... The central act of Hindu worship ... is to stand in the presence of the deity and to behold the image with one's own eyes, to see and be seen by the deity."
    —Diana Eck, *Darsan: Seeing the Divine Image in India* (New York: Columbia University Press, 1998), 3

7   Establishing the kingdom in your own life or in society requires both the teaching, presented in a clear and intelligent manner, and the mind and imagination of the listener. You have to be ready to hear the teaching, let it deepen, and observe it ripen. It would help to have a good sense of the poetic and a willingness to change. The kingdom is like a seed that bears fruit in action. If it is not nurtured and allowed to mature, it could end up as a fruitless effort. It has to be rooted in good ideas, a willingness to change, and the desire to do good or live a good life. It is not enough to go through the motions of conventional religion. Your wish for a utopian world has to be real.

This community's heart has become sluggish.
They don't hear well and their eyes are weak.
Otherwise they could see with their eyes,
Hear with their ears and understand with their hearts,
And they would change and I would cure them.[5]

"But your eyes have been blessed. You can see and your ears can hear. Many prophets and remarkable people yearned to see what you see but didn't see it and to hear what you hear but didn't hear.[6]

"Listen, I'll explain the parable of the sower. If you hear the story about the kingdom and don't understand it, a wicked one may come and take away what was planted in your heart. This is the seed scattered on the road. Some people hear the message and grasp it immediately and are inspired. But since these people have no roots, the effect lasts only a short time. This is the seed that fell on rocky ground. When these people get into trouble or are criticized for this philosophy, they soon drift away.

"The one who received the seeds that fell among brambles is the person who hears about this way of thinking but is choked by the concerns of life and the allure of wealth. This seed doesn't bear any fruit.

"But the one who receives the seeds that fall on good soil is the person who hears the teaching and gets it. He produces a real crop, maybe a hundred, sixty, or thirty times what was sown."[7]

8 Are you wheat—nourishing and real—or a weed? If you are among the
   weeds who just take up space and live unconsciously and absorbed in yourself, you will end up on the compost heap. If you are among the wheat, you
   will be fully present and ready to do your part. The separating is automatic,
   the result of your being and your actions.

9 Many Zen stories tell of *satori*, or transformation, occurring after a simple
   discovery, like seeing some pure aspect of nature. Similarly, entering the
   kingdom is not necessarily the result of a long period of study. The kingdom
   itself may not be like a church or a movement or even a philosophy. It may
   be tiny, like a thought, an inspiration, a point of view, or, perhaps best of
   all, a small turn of imagination. Once you make that turn and understand
   that there is another way to live, one that is open to community through
   love and to a spiritual universe, everything shifts. Birds come to live in it.
   Throughout religious literature birds are images of spirit. A whole world of
   spiritual ideas and values comes to you when you finally leave behind your
   materialism and self-interest.
       It is customary to think of Jesus's teachings as a huge system of thought
   guarded by a mammoth church. But Jesus says it is more like a tiny seed that
   grows modestly. Even your life and personality are tiny seeds that attract the
   world to you.

Jesus presented them with another parable: "The kingdom is like another person who sowed good seeds in his field. But while everyone was asleep, an enemy came and planted weeds among the wheat and went off. Then, when the wheat sprouted and formed heads, the weeds could also be seen.

"The owner's workers came to him and said, 'Didn't you plant good wheat in that field? Then where did these weeds come from?'

"'Some malicious person has done this,' he replied.

"'Would you like us to go and pull them out?'

"'No. When you pull up the weeds you'll also take out the wheat. Let them grow up together until it's time to bring in the wheat. At that point I'll instruct the workers to gather the weeds to be burned and the wheat to be stored in the barn.'"[8]

Then he told them another parable: "The kingdom is like a mustard seed that a person planted in his field. It's the tiniest of all the seeds, but when it matures it's the largest of the garden plants, like a tree. The birds come down from the sky and make nests in its branches."[9]

10 The kingdom is like yeast, that is, something small that makes everything around it larger and more flavorful. The kingdom is a leaven. It is not about creating a life beyond or outside our normal one; rather, it intensifies the world we know. But notice the word "hid." There is something hidden about the kingdom.

New Testament scholar Bernard Brandon Scott says that in the Bible "leaven" often has negative connotations. The kingdom is not always in tune with the normal ways of doing things. Its point of view may be difficult and challenging. Scott tells of a woman with cancer. She said that "the parable had finally allowed her to see that God was on her side even in her battle with cancer" (Scott). Cancer was her yeast, a bad thing that was still a catalyst for personal change.

11 In the larger sense of the word, Jesus is a poet, a spiritual poet, using imagery for the mysteries that he proclaims and embodies. He is often taken too literally as a moralist. For many, reading the Gospels as spiritual poetry would be a crucial move. Notice, by the way, how strong this passage is: Jesus said nothing that was not a story or fiction containing a profound insight. What if we read everything Jesus said as poetic?

12 Psalm 78:2.

13 That is, the end of the period before the kingdom begins to take root. Even now, some people are deciding to live by the values expressed in the Gospels, and some are not. Those who are not are self-selecting a life that is unconscious and lacking a sense of meaning. It is not that they are rejecting the written Gospels or are failing to join a movement; their problem is that they cannot appreciate the points of view and values of the kingdom.

He told them yet another parable: "The kingdom is like yeast that a woman took and hid in sixteen pounds of flour until it rose."10

Jesus always spoke to the people in parables; in fact, he said nothing that was not a parable.11 So the psalmist's words were fulfilled:

> *I will open my mouth in parables.*
> *I will reveal things that have been*
> *hidden since the world's beginning.*12

Then Jesus left the crowd and entered the house. His followers came and said, "Tell us what the parable about the weeds in the field means."

He replied, "The person who planted the good seeds is the son of man. The field represents the world and the good seeds stand for the children of the kingdom. The weeds represent the children of the wicked person. The horrible person who planted them is the devil. The harvest is the end of this era,13 and the farmworkers are messengers.

"Just as the weeds are yanked out and burned up, that's the way it will be in the end. The son of man will send his messengers and they'll weed out anything that makes for wickedness and anyone who is unethical. They'll toss them into the fiery furnace where they will cry out and grit their teeth. Then the ethical people will sparkle like the sun in the kingdom of their father.

14 The idea of the kingdom is the key to happiness, health, and world peace. It is precious. It is worth any cost in material comfort.

15 The kingdom comes at a price. When you discover it and recognize it for what it is, it is worth giving up anything you value for it. Nothing is more important than finally understanding that life only makes sense when we are generous, thoughtful, and instruments of healing.

16 Deciding whether or not to live the values of the kingdom sorts you out. You are either living an ethical, intense, and engaged life, or you are unconscious and lost. Either way, right now, you are judged by your own decision. No one else is condemning or rewarding you. The kingdom implies a choice, and the choice itself evaluates who and what you are.

17 If you are compelled by the spirit of the Gospels, you will have to sort out your old values from the new ones. Oftentimes, people try to do both: live the way they have always done and somehow adapt the Gospel teachings to their lifestyle. But Jesus presents his teachings as more of a challenge. This new way of life does not accept compromise easily. You have to choose one way or the other.

"Listen closely. The kingdom above is like a treasure that lay buried in a field. A person discovered it but then buried it again and then, delighted, went and sold everything he had and bought the field.¹⁴

"Or, the kingdom is like a businessperson in search of precious pearls. When he found one that was worth a great deal, he went and sold everything he had and bought it.¹⁵

"Or, the kingdom is like a net let down into the water, catching every species of fish. When it was full, the fishermen drew it up onto the shore. Then they sat down and put the good fish in baskets and threw the bad ones away.¹⁶

"This is the way it will be at the end. Messengers will appear to separate the ethical from the unethical and throw the latter into a fiery furnace, where they will cry out and clench their teeth.

"Do you understand all this?"

"Yes," they said.

He told them, "Every enlightened person who has learned about the kingdom is like the owner of a house who takes both the new and the old out of storage."¹⁷

When Jesus finished with these parables, he left the area. When he arrived in his own country, he taught in the synagogue and the people were shocked. "Where did he get this wisdom and these powers? Isn't this the carpenter's son? Isn't his mother's name Mary? Aren't his brothers James, Joseph, Simon, and Judas? Aren't all his sisters here among us? Where did this man get all this wisdom?"

18 Good people with good ideas can be threatening because they upset our comfort with the way we have been living and thinking. Sometimes we attack them by challenging the person rather than the idea. This is called the *ad hominem* argument: criticizing the person rather than sorting out the ideas. We may go a step further and ostracize or banish the person, again with the hope of distancing ourselves from the idea. Or someone among us may beat up or even kill the person—consider John Kennedy or Martin Luther King—as a way to avoid the challenge. Friends, family members, and neighbors may find it especially difficult to tolerate a challenging idea from someone they know.

They weren't happy with him.

Jesus said, "In his own country and his own house, a prophet doesn't get any respect."[18]

He didn't manifest the power of his thought there because the people didn't put any faith in him.

1   In his play *Salomé*, Oscar Wilde dramatically draws out the contrast between the ascetic John and the Venus-like Salomé. Herod says, "I have looked at you all this evening. Your beauty troubled me. Your beauty has grievously troubled me, and I have looked at you too much." Wilde sees a conflict here between purity and sensuality, a polarization you do not see in Jesus. Herod is troubled, while Jesus is composed. Jesus is highly spiritual and at the same time quite sensual, loving food, the company of friends, oil massage, and, according to the Gnostic Gospels' *Acts of John*, dancing.

Chapter 14

Herod, who was ruling at the time, received a report about Jesus and had an explanation: "This is John the Baptist, come to life. That's why he has special powers."

Previously, Herod had taken John and put him in chains and then in prison, all because of Herodias, his brother Philip's wife. John had told him that it wasn't legal for him to be with her. Herod thought of killing John, but he was afraid of the people—they thought of John as a prophet.

On the occasion of Herod's birthday, Herodias's daughter danced for them¹ and delighted Herod so much that he vowed to give her whatever she wanted. Prodded by her mother, she made her request—the head of John the Baptist on a platter. This request disturbed the king, but because of the promises he had made and with his dinner guests right in front of him, he gave the order and had John beheaded in prison. They brought the head in on a platter and gave it to the girl and she brought it to her mother. John's followers came and retrieved his body and buried it. Then they went and told Jesus.

2   Jesus goes back and forth from the thick of society to the solitude of the desert. He goes by boat, like Tristan, a hero of Celtic mythology who casts his fate to the sea, and St. Brendan, who leaves Iona for Ireland on a spiritual journey. Jesus also echoes the sea-journey of the sun, the image of the hero's trek across the earth. He is peripatetic, in motion, on land and sea, constantly moving, a spiritual leader for the entire world. He is a walker and a sailor, but not a landowner. This does not mean that it is literally wrong to own land but that, metaphorically, everyone is a saunterer, if only in his mind, always in movement, ever on the journey, constantly a seeker.

3   This translation renders *therapeia* as "tended" rather than "miraculously healed," presenting to some an unfamiliar picture of Jesus. To some extent he is a miracle worker but also a man with a very big heart and an extraordinary capacity for compassion. The word "tended" here is more faithful to the Greek than "miraculously healed."

4   This is one of many passing references to the sky (*ouranos*), the Ouranic mystery by which a spiritual and cosmic viewpoint is an essential part of the Jesus way. In his "kingdom" you find a constant and vibrant relationship to the sky mysteries. You do not get lost in your own earthly concerns, although they are also important. The two go together: the cosmos and your local life, your spirituality and your everyday world.

5   Jesus sometimes describes his teachings as food. Clearly, they are food for the soul and spirit. Here we see a follow-up to the parables that describes the kingdom as something small but powerful. He has only a few fish and some bread, but feeds a great number of people. The Jesus approach is not complicated. Basically, it involves a shift away from narcissism, to a lifestyle of love and respect, dealing with demonic passions, and healing and caring for those who are suffering. With these few principles, just a few fish sandwiches, you can change the world.

When Jesus heard about these events, he left by boat[2] and went alone to a desert area. The people got wind of this and followed him on foot out of the towns. When he got to the shore, he saw the big crowd and felt sorry for them and tended[3] their sick ones.

At evening time, his followers approached him and said, "This is a remote place and it's late. Dismiss the people so they can go to the towns and buy some food." Jesus said, "They don't have to go. Give them something to eat."

"All we have with us are five loaves of bread and two fish."

"Bring them over here."

Then he asked the people to sit on the grass. He took the five loaves of bread and the two fish and looked up to the sky.[4] He blessed the loaves and broke them into pieces and gave them to his followers and they gave them to the people. Everyone ate and felt satisfied and picked up the leftovers and filled twelve baskets. About five thousand men, women, and children had eaten.[5]

6 "And Jesus was a sailor when he walked upon the water ...," as Leonard
Cohen puts it in his song "Suzanne."

The story of Jesus walking on the water has gripped people for millennia.
It is not just proof of Jesus's power, but also a strong image. When you leave
behind the pragmatic, literal, and solely material world of ordinary culture
and have a vision and a utopian ideal for humanity, you can do things that
are simply not possible in the ordinary realm. You may not literally walk
on water, but you are not limited by what is reasonable, known, and easily
explained. Many religions of the world understand this, while Christianity, so adapted to modern thinking, has neglected it: People who discover
the laws of life, as Jesus has, have powers not available to others. One is an
extraordinary capacity to heal.

7 "Trust is the door to the alternative reality that is God's domain. The word
we formerly used for trust was faith. But faith has been spoiled by its popular
connotations, intellectual assent to the standard doctrine of one's religious
tradition.... Trust does not involve believing something or in something.
Trust involves seeing the world and other people for what they are when
viewed through God's eyes."

—Robert W. Funk, *A Credible Jesus: Fragments of a Vision* (Salem, OR: Polebridge
Press, 2002), 31

Or, another way of saying this: Extraordinary trust in life gives you extraordinary personal power.

8 Jesus heals with his person and his presence. You need only get close to
him and you are better. This is a model for how Jesus's followers could be.
It is not enough to stuff your head with beliefs and teachings. You have to
become a different kind of person, one who is suffused with the imagination
of life we find in the Gospels.

At that point he asked his followers to get into the boat and go on to the other side, while he said good-bye to the people. After he had done that, he went up the mountain alone to pray. By evening he was entirely by himself, but by now the waves had swept the boat away from land, for the wind had turned against it. In the morning he came toward them walking on the lake.[6]

When his followers saw him walking on the water, they were terrified and said, "It's a mirage," and they cried out in fear.

But Jesus assured them, "Be strong. It's me. Don't be afraid."

Peter replied, "Sir, if it's you, tell me if it's all right to come to you on the water."

He said, "Come on, then."

Peter got out of the boat and started walking on the water toward Jesus. But then he felt the force of the strong wind and was frightened and began to sink. He shouted out, "Master, save me." Quickly Jesus stretched out his hand and grabbed hold of him.

"Your trust isn't strong enough," Jesus said. "Why did you doubt?"[7]

When they got into the boat, the wind died down and those already in the boat bowed to him. "It's true that you are a son of God."

When they completed the crossing they were in Gennesaret, where the people there recognized him and spread the word everywhere and brought all their sick to him. They asked if they could just brush against the edge of his garment, and everyone who touched him got better.[8]

1   Isaiah 29:13. Another constant theme in the Gospels: Some ideas and actions
     come from human reasoning and others come from a deeply spiritual source.
     This difference comes to the foreground in John's Gospel where Jesus fre-
     quently reminds his audience that he does not speak for himself but rather
     the Father is speaking through him.

Chapter 15

S ome Pharisees and intellectuals from Jerusalem came to Jesus and asked him, "Why do your followers disregard the traditions of our elders? For instance, they don't wash their hands before eating."

Jesus replied, "Well, why do your people, too, in the name of your tradition, break God's rule? God said to honor your father and mother and that anyone who curses them should be put to death. But you say that a person can tell his father or mother, 'Listen, whatever support you might have had from me I'm now going to offer up as a sacrifice to God.' Then he doesn't have to honor his father. So, calling on tradition, you negate the word of God. Hypocrites. Isaiah was right in predicting your behavior:

> *These people honor me with their lips*
> *But their hearts are miles away from me.*
> *They devote themselves to me pointlessly*
> *Because their teachings are self-centered."* [1]

Jesus summoned the people to him and said, "Listen closely and try to understand. It isn't what goes into a person's mouth that makes him unclean, but what comes out. That makes him unclean."

His followers approached him later and said, "Are you aware that the Pharisees were upset when they heard you say this?"

He said, "Every plant that my father above has not planted will be pulled up. Steer clear of them. They are the blind leading the blind. If a blind person guides a blind person, they'll both fall into a hole."

2 What counts is not the formalities of religion and rules that you observe, but the state of your soul and how you act from it. Rituals are important for keeping your imagination rich and your mind alert for living effectively. But rituals can become empty, and then it is most important to keep your vision alive and live your exceptional values. There is a reformer aspect to Jesus and therefore to his teachings.

3 This Canaanite woman is another outsider who can understand the values of the kingdom. Today it may appear that only Christians are invited into the Jesus kingdom. But the Gospels show again and again that the outsider may have a deeper trust and therefore more profoundly has a place in the kingdom. The Gospels have a special home in Christianity, historically, but they do not belong to it exclusively.

Peter said, "Explain this parable to us."

He said, "You still don't get it? Can't you see that whatever goes into the mouth enters the stomach and goes out into the toilet? But what comes out of the mouth originates in the heart, and this is what pollutes a person. For out of the heart come bad thoughts, murder, adultery, sexual transgressions, thieving, lies, and slander. These are the things that truly pollute a person, but eating without washing your hands doesn't."[2]

Jesus left there and went off to Tyre and Sidon and those areas. A Canaanite woman from the region came along and cried out, "Be so kind as to help me, sir, son of David. My daughter is in a terrible condition. She's possessed."

He didn't say a word.

His followers came over to him and pressed him, "Send her away. She keeps screaming at us."

He answered, "I was not sent to tend only the lost sheep of the house of Israel."[3]

She came and bent down in front of him. "Help me, sir."

He said, "It isn't right to take the children's bread and toss it to the dogs."

"Yes, sir," she said, "but dogs eat the bits that fall off the master's table."

Jesus replied, "Woman, you have such deep trust that your wish will be granted." Her daughter got better that very hour.

Jesus left there and walked along the Sea of Galilee and then climbed up a mountainside and sat down. Large crowds came to him bringing people who couldn't walk, the visually impaired, the disabled, those with speech disorders, and many others. They positioned them at his feet and he tended them. The

4   It would indeed be a miracle if we could solve global hunger even in times of economic distress. The miracle takes place in soup kitchens and other poorly funded organizations that recognize the importance of food. Throughout the Gospels we see Jesus concerned about food, for himself and others. To be in the kingdom means to be sensitive to the importance of food and eating, not just for the body but also for the soul and spirit. A modern reader might understand this story as proof of Jesus's validity and divinity, but the teaching clearly is about compassion and feeding the hungry. It is also yet another image for how the kingdom is made of small nourishing elements, perhaps a life well lived with friends and family.

people were amazed when they saw these people speak, the sick get healthy, walk, and recover their vision. They praised the God of Israel.

Jesus called his followers to him and said, "I'm concerned for these people who have been with me for three days and have had nothing to eat. I don't want to send them away hungry or they may faint on their journey."

His followers said, "Where could we possibly get enough bread in this remote place to feed this crowd?"

"How many loaves of bread do you have?" Jesus asked.

"Seven," they said. "And a few little fish."

He told the people to sit on the ground and then took the seven loaves and the fish. After giving thanks, he broke them into pieces and gave them to his followers and they passed them on to the people. Everyone ate and was satisfied. Afterward, the followers gathered up seven baskets of leftovers. Four thousand people had eaten.[4] After dismissing the crowd, Jesus got in a boat and headed for the region of Magadan.

1   Once again Jesus encourages us to think poetically and read the signs all
    around us; to use our intuition and change the way we live. If we see vio-
    lence and greed ingrained in our world, then we know the direction to take
    to reform it.

    The Hebrew Bible story of Jonah tells of a man who refuses the call to
    wake people up morally. He spends three days inside a great fish, which
    then spews him back onto land, and Jonah fulfills his mission. It is our job, as
    it was Jesus's, to come out of our passivity and speak out against corruption
    and violence.

2   The story of the miracle of the loaves is not about actual bread. Just as the
    yeast of the Pharisees is a problem, the bread Jesus produces is bread in the
    sense of the teachings. In another context Jesus says, "I am the bread of life."
    The kingdom is like a tiny mustard seed or a little yeast in a mass of flour,
    and it is also like a few fish sandwiches for five thousand people. It consists
    of just a few clues on how to live, but those hints and the basic vision are
    sufficient. We need nourishment for the tasks of rebuilding the world on a
    foundation of higher values, but the simple teachings of the Gospels sustain
    us better than elaborate rules and complicated theologies.

Chapter 16

The Pharisees and the Sadducees came to check Jesus out. They asked him to show them a sign from the sky.

He said, "When evening arrives, you say, 'The sky is red, so we're going to have good weather.' In the morning, you say, 'The sky is overcast. It's going to be a stormy day.' You know how to interpret conditions in the sky but not the signs of the times. A wicked and adulterous generation asks for a sign, but the only one it will get is the sign of Jonah."[1]

Jesus left them and went away.

When they crossed the lake, the followers forgot to pack some bread. "Take care," Jesus said to them. "Be aware of the yeast of the Pharisees and the Sadducees."

They had a discussion about his warning: "It must have to do with the fact that we didn't bring any bread."

Overhearing the conversation, Jesus said, "You don't trust enough. What are you talking about? Not having bread? Don't you understand yet? Remember five loaves for five thousand people? How many baskets of leftovers? Or the seven loaves for the four thousand? How many leftovers? Can't you understand that I wasn't talking about bread? Be aware of the yeast of the Pharisees and the Sadducees."[2]

Finally they understood that he wasn't talking about bread and yeast but rather the teachings of the Pharisees and the Sadducees.

3 "The original meaning of *ekklesia,* 'church,' was not a hyper-organization of spiritual functionaries. It denoted a community gathering at a particular place at a particular time for a particular action.... Every local church makes the whole church fully present."
    —Hans Küng, *The Catholic Church: A Short History,* translated by John Bowden (New York: Modern Library, 2003), 5

The images of a mustard seed and a small amount of yeast apply to community. You do not need a huge group of people. Maybe a small community would be more appropriate as an experiment in living the kingdom today.

4 Peter now has a way of dealing with matters of the kingdom, but this has to do with the spiritual realm, the kingdom of the sky, not a temporal kingdom. We, too, are more in need of a spiritual sense of connection with all of humanity than a physical gathering of like-minded people.

When Jesus entered the district of Caesarea Philippi, he quizzed his followers. "Who do people say the son of man is?"

They answered, "Some say John the Baptist. Others, Elijah. Others, Jeremiah or one of the prophets." He said to them, "But what about you? Who would you say I am?" Simon Peter answered, "You are Christos, the living son of God." Jesus answered him, "You will find happiness, Simon bar Jona. Flesh and blood hasn't taught you this, but rather my father who is everywhere.

"Let me say this: 'You are Peter, and on this rock I will create my community,³ and the gates of Hades will not overpower it. I will give you the keys to the spiritual kingdom.⁴ Whatever you ban on the earth will be banned in the sky and whatever you allow on the earth will be allowed in the sky.'"

Then he sternly instructed his followers not to tell anyone that he was Christos, the anointed one.

From that time on, Jesus began to explain to his students that he would go to Jerusalem and suffer a great deal from the elders, the religious leaders, and the teachers, and that he would perish and come back to life on the third day.

Peter took him aside and complained, "No, sir. This will never happen to you."

Jesus turned to Peter and said, "Back off, Satan. You're in my way. You're speaking as a human being, not on behalf of God."

5 The soul is the important thing. Wealth and other life concerns have their place but are much lower on the list of priorities. Jesus offers a soul-centered way of life, an alternative to plain earthly values. Still, you never hear him speak in a purely otherworldly manner. He unites earth and sky. These two images carry equal weight and appear frequently in the Gospels. In the long philosophical tradition after Jesus, soul is the middle ground between matter and spirit.

Then Jesus addressed his followers, "If someone wants to join me, he has to forget his own interests, pick up his cross, and follow me. Whoever wants to save his soul will lose it. Whoever loses his soul for my sake will recover it. What good is it for a person to acquire the whole world and yet do harm to his soul? What can take the place of a person's soul?[5]

"The son of man will appear amid all his father's magnificence and with his attendants. Then he will reward each person according to his actions. Now I can finally tell you: Some of you standing here right now will not taste death until you see the son of man coming into his kingdom."

1   This image of Christos as more than human, a mythic figure, shamanic, a figure of the imagination, is an essential aspect of the Gospels. If we do not keep in mind this metamorphosis of the man Jesus into the spiritual Christos, we tend to anthropomorphize the entire story and finally literalize it all, thus losing the mystery and the essence of who Jesus was and what he was talking about. The Gospels apparently contain history, but they are also mystical poetry. In William Blake's words from "Laocoön," "The Eternal Body of Man is The Imagination, God himself, that is, The Divine Body, Jesus we are his Members."

2   It is only in the resurrection, the essential mystery of the Gospels, that the essence of Jesus is revealed. The great metamorphosis on the mountain foreshadows the risen Christos, not just a human being but a crucial figure of spiritual fantasy, a vision, an inner model for all of humanity.

Chapter 17

Six days later Jesus gathered Peter, James, and John, and James's brother, and led them, a select group, up a high mountain. There he shape-shifted right in front of them. His face glowed like the sun and his garments were as white as light.[1] Suddenly Moses and Elijah appeared in front of them in conversation with him.

Peter said to Jesus, "Sir, it's good that we're here. If you would like, I'll set up three tents, one for you, one for Moses, and one for Elijah."

As he was talking, a bright, glowing cloud engulfed them and a voice from the mist said, "This is my son. I love him. He gives me unimaginable pleasure. Listen to him."

When the followers heard this, they fell down on their faces, overcome by fear. But Jesus came and touched them. "Get up," he said. "Don't be afraid." When they looked up, they saw no one but Jesus.

Coming down the mountain, Jesus warned them, "Don't tell anyone about this vision until the son of man has risen from the dead."[2]

The students asked him, "Why do the learned say that Elijah has to come beforehand?"

Jesus replied, "Certainly, Elijah has to come first and restore everything. But I can tell you that Elijah has already come, and they didn't recognize him. They did what they wanted with him, and the son of man is going to suffer at their hands in a similar fashion." Then the students realized that he was speaking to them about John the Baptist.

3   "Corrupt" in the sense of profoundly misguided. People still cannot appreci-
     ate the level of reality Jesus's actions point to. It is clear in the Book of John
     that when you see Jesus you are seeing the one who sent him, an unimagin-
     ably deep, mysterious, and archetypal reality that accounts for our lives but
     is never equivalent to any reductive idea of a mere person. Jesus, the poet
     savior, can be fully appreciated only with a poetic imagination.

4   Walter Burkert, the esteemed historian of Greek religion, defines "daimon"
     briefly this way: "Daimon is occult power, a force that drives a person for-
     ward where no agent can be named. The individual feels as it were that the
     tide is with him, he acts with the daimon, or else when everything turns
     against him, he stands against the daimon.... Illness may be described as 'a
     hated daimon' that assails the sufferer.... There is no image of a daimon, and
     there is no cult" (Burkert).

5   The currency of the kingdom is trust. Even a small amount goes a long way.
     Not faith as belief or theology, but faith as trust. Notice, too, another refer-
     ence to a mustard seed as something very small. Earlier we saw the mustard
     seed as an image of the kingdom; here it represents the power of even a
     small degree of trust.

When they approached the crowd, a man came to Jesus and bowed to him. "Sir, would you be so kind to look at my son? He has seizures related to mental illness and is suffering tremendously. Often he falls into fire or water. I brought him to your students, but they couldn't do anything for him."

Jesus spoke, "What an untrusting and corrupt people.³ How much longer do I have to be with you and deal with you? Bring him to me."

Jesus rebuked the daimon⁴ and it came out of him and the child got better right away.

The students approached Jesus privately and said, "Why couldn't we get rid of it?"

He said to them, "Because your trust isn't great enough. I'm always telling you, if you have trust the size of a mustard seed, say to a mountain, 'Move from here to over there,' and it will move. Nothing will be impossible for you."⁵

When they were staying all together in Galilee, Jesus said to them, "The son of man will be betrayed into the hands of people who will kill him, and on the third day he will arise." They became very sad.

6 Here Jesus links the magical and miraculous style of the kingdom with the very worldly and ordinary need to pay taxes. Everything is redeemable in the imagination of the kingdom.

When they reached Capernaum, collectors of the two-drachma tax approached Peter and asked, "Does your teacher pay the two drachmas?"

"Yes, he does," he answered.

When Peter came home, Jesus spoke first, "What do you think, Simon? Who do you think the world's leaders collect their taxes from, their own children or others?"

"Others," Peter answered.

"Then the children are exempt," Jesus said. "But so that we don't break any of their rules, go to the lake and toss in your line. Take the first fish you catch, open its mouth, and find a four-drachma coin. Take it and give it to them as payment for my tax and yours."[6]

1 Typical adult perception and understanding cannot gain access to the king-dom. On the other hand, a child's point of view, so different, so uncontami-nated by adult interpretations and values, has a good chance.

"The Aion is a child playing, moving pieces on a board game. The kingdom is a child's."
—Herakleitos, early Greek philosopher

2 Children are closer to their mysterious origin from above. Adults have lost contact with it. Children have a guardian in constant relationship with the supreme realm of spirit, with the source of life. We adults not only have to be reborn but we also have to think and act like children. This is perhaps more than and yet similar to the Zen notion of beginner's mind, never losing the sense that you are always learning, always starting fresh.

Chapter 18

One time the followers approached Jesus and asked, "Who is greatest in the kingdom?" He called to a child and asked him to stand in the middle of them. Then he said, "What I'm saying is that unless you change and become like children you will never enter the kingdom. Whoever welcomes one child like this in my name welcomes me.[1] But if anyone stands between one of these little ones and me, he'd be better off having a huge stone tied around his neck and being dumped deep in the sea.

"It's a sad day for the world when people are persuaded to do wrong. It happens all the time, yet I pity the man who is the cause of it. If your hand or foot entices you to do wrong, cut it off and throw it away. It would be better to be disabled than to have two good hands and feet and be thrown into never-ending fire. And if your eye is the source of your mischief, pluck it out and toss it. It's preferable to have one eye than to have two and be thrown into the fire of Gehenna.

"Make sure you don't belittle even one ordinary person. I assure you that people's guardians are always gazing at the face of my father in the sky.[2] But what's your opinion? Say a man owns a hundred sheep and one wanders off. Won't he leave the ninety-nine on the hills to search for the one that's missing? If he finds it, I think he'll be happier for that one sheep than for the ninety-nine that didn't wander off. In the same spirit, your father in the sky doesn't want any of the 'insignificant' ones to be lost.

"If your brother wrongs you, go and discuss it with him, just the two of you. If he listens to you, you have gained a brother. If

3   Here is another radical plank in the platform of the kingdom: If two or more
    people have come together in the spirit of the kingdom, of course the Father
    is present and engaged. There is potency in small communities dedicated
    to high values. The Sky Father keeps the imagination fixed on transcendent
    and sublime values. If people gather to discuss and foster those values, the
    spirit of the Father, whom Jesus always has in mind, will be present.

    The Jesus way is quite worldly; it is all about enjoying life and living with
    an open heart. When you do this, the deeper cosmic laws of life, in the
    hands of the Father, lie just beneath the surface.

he doesn't listen to you, take one or two others with you. Every serious matter should be attested by two or three witnesses. If he still doesn't listen, tell the community. If he doesn't listen to the community, then he's like someone outside the community, like a public functionary. I assure you, whatever you disallow on earth will be forbidden in the sky, and whatever you approve on earth will be allowed in the sky.

"Another thing: If two of you agree about something you want to ask for on earth, my father above will do it for you. Where two or three come together in my name, I am right there with them."[3]

Peter came and said to him, "Sir, if another member of the community does something to offend me, how many times should I forgive him? Seven times?"

Jesus said to him, "Not seven times, seventy-seven times.

"That's why the kingdom is like a king who wanted to settle accounts with his servants. As he was starting the process, one came before him owing ten thousand talents, or thousands of dollars. Since he couldn't pay, the master ordered that he be sold, along with his wife and children and all his things, and payment be made. The servant fell to his knees and pleaded, 'Be patient with me and I'll pay you everything.' Out of pity the master forgave him the debt and let him go. The same servant, going out, bumped into one of his fellow servants who owed him a hundred denarii, or a few dollars. He grabbed him by the throat and said, 'Pay what you owe.' His fellow servant got down and pleaded, 'Be patient and I'll pay you.' He refused and threw him into prison until he paid the debt. When the other servants saw what had taken place, they reported it to the

4   Remember that the parables describe the new kingdom or world of values
    that Jesus recommends. Here, we see a psychological pattern that is com-
    mon and yet difficult to understand. People who have suffered abuse do not
    usually treat others kindly but rather abuse them the way they were abused.
    Abuse gives rise to abuse. But if you truly want the reward of being in the
    kingdom of the sky that Jesus describes in his teachings, you have to get out
    of this pattern and instead treat others differently from the way you were
    treated. This is not easy because it may be an automatic response to do unto
    others what was done unto you. You have to use your intelligence, become
    convinced of Jesus's psychology and end the pattern of repeated abuse. For-
    giveness is one of the building blocks of the kingdom.

master. The master summoned him and said, 'You're worthless. I forgave all your debt because you pleaded with me. Shouldn't you have been kind to your fellow servant as I was kind to you?' The master handed him over to be tortured until he paid his debt fully. My father above will do the same to all of you, if you don't forgive your brother from your heart."[4]

1   You have to read this passage on divorce carefully. Jesus is defining marriage
    in the kingdom. It is not a human arrangement. It goes infinitely deep, if, I
    would add, it is a real marriage of souls. If you are aiming at a utopian life in
    a visionary culture, then you do not treat divorce lightly. You consider the
    sacredness of the marriage and how it is the result of forces beyond your
    control. You have profound respect for it and, to that extent, divorce does
    not really separate you. Do not get divorced for any surface reason. Also,
    understand that even after a formal divorce you are still wedded to this per-
    son in a timeless way.

Chapter 19

When Jesus had finished saying these things, he left Galilee and went to the part of Judea that is beyond the Jordan. Large crowds followed him and he cared for them.

Pharisees came to test him and asked, "Is it legal for a man to divorce his wife for any reason?"

"Don't you know," he replied, "that at the beginning the creator made them male and female and said, 'This is why a man will leave his mother and father and join with his wife and the two will be as one body'? So they will no longer be two, but one. What God has put together, no human being should take apart."

"Then why did Moses teach that a man can give his wife divorce papers and leave her?"

Jesus answered, "Moses allowed you to divorce your wives because your hearts were tough. At the beginning it wasn't like this. In my opinion, anyone who divorces his wife, except for serious sexual misconduct, and then marries someone else, commits adultery."[1]

His followers said, "If this is how it is between a husband and wife, it's better not to get married."

"Only those who are given this teaching can handle not being married. Some are constitutionally not suited to marriage. Some are physically unsuited. Others have decided against marriage because of the kingdom, but only those who can handle it should be single."

Then they brought children to Jesus so he could put his hands on them and pray. But his followers complained to those who had brought them.

2   The Tao Te Ching contrasts the way of worldly wisdom with the way of the
child:

> "But I alone am drifting, not knowing where I am
> Like a newborn babe before it learns to smile."
> —Lao Tzu, *Tao Te Ching*, translated by Gia-Fu Feng and Jane English (New
> York: Vintage, 1972), 20

In context, this "drifting" is a good thing—being sustained by the maternal
aspect of life and trusting in it.

3   "Sky" is an image that Jesus often uses in referring to the spiritual realm.
Sometimes he contrasts the kingdom of the sky with mere human, unconscious values. Here the meaning is clear: Do not measure your happiness
by the extent of your possessions but by your ideals, values, and degree of
compassion.

4   Jesus's close circle of followers and admirers did indeed leave everything and
place their trust in him. But, as always, the reward for choosing the kingdom
is immediate. You find this new level of experience, and at that moment you
are in a different position in life. Your rewards are not temporary; they are
immaterial and lasting.

Jesus said, "Let the children come to me. Don't stand in their way. The kingdom is for them."[2] After he had placed his hands on them, he went on from there.

A man approached Jesus and asked, "What good work should I do to merit eternal life?"

"Why do you ask me about the good?" Jesus replied. "There is only one good. If you want to really be alive, observe the commandments."

"Which ones?" the man asked.

"Don't commit murder, adultery, theft, or perjury. Honor your father and mother and love your neighbor as yourself."

The young man said, "I've kept all these. Am I missing something?"

Jesus answered, "If you want to really do it, go and sell your possessions and give them to the poor. You will have treasure in the sky.[3] Then come and join me."

When the young man heard this, he went away unhappy because he had extensive property.

Jesus addressed his followers, "I know, it isn't easy for a wealthy person to enter the kingdom. It's easier for a camel to pass through the eye of a needle than for a rich man to enter the kingdom of God."

When the followers heard this, they were shocked. They said, "Then who can be assured a place?"

Jesus looked at them and said, "From the human perspective, it can't be done. But to God, anything is possible."

Peter said, "We have left everything and joined up with you. What will we have?"[4]

5   What Jesus offers in his promise of the kingdom is a life different from the one we know as our everyday effort to raise our families and survive financially. The kingdom is all about timeless matters, and when we can adjust our thinking to live in eternity as well as in time, we will find unexpected joy. We will have an authority in life that is very different from the worldly powers of finance and government and business hierarchies. In a memorable summary, Jesus says, "Ones at the bottom will be on top."

Here is a parallel teaching from Zen master Shunryu Suzuki that may help elucidate Jesus's important teaching: "Sometimes a man bows to a woman; sometimes a woman bows to a man. Sometimes the disciple bows to the master; sometimes the master bows to the disciple. A master who cannot bow to his disciple cannot bow to Buddha. Sometimes the master and disciple bow together to Buddha. Sometimes we may bow to cats and dogs" (Suzuki).

Jesus said, "I'll tell you. At the time of the great change, when the son of man sits on the throne of glory, you who joined with me will also sit on twelve thrones, judging the twelve tribes of Israel. Anyone who left a house or brothers and sisters or mother and father for my sake will have a hundred times as much and will enjoy eternity on earth. Many on top will find themselves on the bottom, and the ones at the bottom will be on top."[5]

1   This phrase in Greek reads literally "wicked eye," which may be something like a "hard heart," a body feature describing someone who cannot be open to others.

2   The logic of the kingdom is different from ordinary human logic. What seems just and reasonable to the ordinary person may be contradicted in the kingdom—such as loving your enemies. The rule of the kingdom is a reverse logic, or a logic of reversal. It does not divide people into hierarchies but is radically democratic. What you gain by being part of the kingdom is not the usual physical comforts or prestige but a sense of purpose. And you do not gain this because of how much effort you put into it but simply because you choose to live this way.

Sufis tell a similar story about the mullah Nasrudin. He wanted to take music lessons and asked a teacher how much they would cost. "Ten dollars for the first lesson and five dollars a lesson after that." "Fine," said Nasrudin. "I'll start with the second lesson."

Chapter 20

"The kingdom is like the master of a house who went out early in the morning to hire workers for his vineyard. They agreed on a denarius per day and the workers went into the vineyard. At the third hour, nine o'clock, he went out and saw others standing around in the market square doing nothing. He said to them, 'Why don't you, too, go and work in my vineyard? I'll pay you whatever is appropriate.' So they went out.

"He went again at the sixth hour and the ninth hour and found yet more standing around. He said, 'Why have you been standing around doing nothing all day long?'

"'No one has hired us,' they answered.

"He said, 'Then why don't you go into the vineyard, too?'

"When evening came, the owner said to his manager, 'Call the workers in and give them their pay. Begin with the ones who were hired last and then go on to the ones hired earlier.'

"The workers who came on in the eleventh hour came and each got a denarius. When the ones who had been hired early came, they thought they'd be paid more. But each of them also got a denarius. They took it but then grumbled about the owner. 'These men who came on last only worked an hour,' they said, 'and yet you have treated them just like us. We've done most of the work and had to withstand the heat of the day, too.'

"He said to this one, 'My friend, I'm not being unfair to you. Didn't you agree to work for a denarius? Take your pay and leave. I want to give the man who was hired last the same as you got. Can't I do what I want with what is mine? Do you have a bad attitude?[1] I mean, are you lacking in generosity?'

"The last will be first, and the first last."[2]

3   Here is another difficult lesson that distinguishes the way of the kingdom
    from ordinary ways of doing things. The decision about who is great or
    honored or in power is made according to high spiritual laws. You could say
    that it is a mystery that life itself decides. Who is to say who rises to the top
    and who remains among the ordinary people? In this sense, the kingdom is a
    non-ego kind of society. Perhaps it is similar to the Dalai Lama being chosen
    by dream and trance or, as the Tao Te Ching teaches, "The sage does not
    attempt anything very big, and thus achieves greatness" (Feng and English).

4   This is an important reversal: Just as "the last will be first," leaders will be ser-
    vants. The way of the world is graft and oppression; the way of the kingdom
    is service. Again, the Tao Te Ching: "If the sage would guide the people, he
    must serve with humility. If he would lead them, he must follow behind"
    (Feng and English). This is a crucial law of the spiritual life: Honor comes
    from service and humility.

As Jesus was going to Jerusalem he drew his twelve followers aside and said to them, "We are going to Jerusalem. The son of man will be betrayed to the leaders and legalists. They will condemn him to death and turn him over to the people at large to be taunted, tortured, and crucified. Then on the third day he'll rise."

Then the mother of Zebedee's sons came to Jesus with one of them and, bowing, asked a favor.

"What do you want?" he asked.

"Allow one of my sons," she said, "to sit to your right and one on your left in your kingdom."

"You don't know what you're asking for," Jesus said to the brothers. "Can you drink the cup I am going to drink?"

"Yes, we can," they replied.

"Yes, you'll drink my cup," Jesus said, "but as to who sits at my right or left, it isn't up to me to grant. It all depends on what my father has decided."[3]

When the ten others heard about all this, they were upset with the brothers. Jesus called them together and said, "You're aware that the leaders of the world tyrannize their people. But this isn't to be your way. No, whoever wants to become great among you has to be your servant, and whoever wants to be first has to be your slave. It's like the son of man. He didn't come to be waited on, but to serve. He offers his life as a ransom for many people."[4]

As Jesus and his followers left Jericho, a large group of people followed him. Two blind men were sitting at the side of the road. They heard Jesus going by and yelled out, "Sir, son of David, help us."

5   Remember the Gospel law of the parable: Every story has layers of meaning.
     Here we should think of getting our sight back not in physical terms but as
     finally seeing how life works.

The people scolded them and told them to hush, but they yelled out all the more loudly, "Sir, son of David, help us."

Jesus stopped and spoke to them. "What do you want me to do?"

"Sir, we want to see."[5]

Jesus felt for them and touched their eyes. Immediately they got their sight back and joined him.

1 Zechariah 9:9.

2 "The opposition between the horse of warfare and the humble, agricultural ass is commonplace in biblical language. From the point of view of the Gospel narrative, then, Christos demonstrates the uselessness of imperial parades by doing an anti-imperial adventus seated on the least military of all beasts, a farmer's ass."
    —Thomas F. Matthews, *The Clash of Gods: A Reinterpretation of Early Christian Art* (Princeton, NJ: Princeton University Press, 1993), 45

There is something about the Jesus way that mocks some ordinary human values and customs. Jesus on the ass is a good example.

Chapter 21

They drew near to Jerusalem and arrived at Bethphage at the Mount of Olives. Jesus sent two of the followers on ahead, telling them, "Go into the village ahead of you, and immediately you'll find a donkey tied up there. Her colt will be next to her. Untie them and bring them to me. If anyone says anything to you, just say that the master needs them, and he will let you take them."

This all happened so that the prophecy would be fulfilled:

> *Tell the daughter of Sion*
> *Look, your king is coming to you,*
> *unassuming, riding on a donkey,*
> *on a colt, the offspring of a donkey.* [1]

The students went and did what Jesus had told them to do. They brought the donkey and colt and put their coats on them, and had Jesus sit on the donkey. [2] A large crowd of people spread their clothes on the road, while others cut branches off the trees and piled them on the path. The crowd that preceded him and those following shouted,

> *Hosanna to the son of David.*
> *Praise to the man who is here in the Lord's name.*
> *Hosanna in the highest.*

When he entered Jerusalem, the whole city was unsettled. People were asking, "Who is this?"

Others responded, "It's Jesus, the prophet from Nazareth in Galilee."

3   The whole point of the kingdom is that it is in our midst and inside us. Jesus brings to an end the notion of religion as a particular place of worship, where spiritual activity goes on in the manner of the marketplace—the religious institution as a business. No, the kingdom is not for those who expect to be chosen because of their virtue or those who are connected to a religious organization. His message is a radical one. The kingdom is inside you and all around you.

4   Again, the child theme is central in the Gospel story. One way to understand it is simple: The kingdom is an alternative way of thinking and living that stands in complete contrast to the worldview and values of society as we know it. Why is it surprising that praise is coming from the mouths of children? Because they are not yet initiated fully into society. They are outsiders of a sort and therefore can speak more directly for the values of the kingdom.

5   Sentimental notions of Jesus are so common that his strong magic against the fig tree may appear harsh. We might consider that the kingdom is serious business. It is about happiness and depression and war and peace. If you read the Gospels without the sentimental prejudice, you may see and appreciate the tough side of Jesus. Religious formalism and judgmental hierarchies have not established the kingdom of the sky but rather an earthly, egoistic version. Symbolically, Jesus curses the fig tree, in place of tradition, for not providing "fruit."

6   Worldly values are often rooted in cynicism, fear, and uncertainty, always in search of factual proof that never fully satisfies. In the kingdom one learns to trust and live without fear.

Jesus arrived at the temple area and threw out everyone buying and selling things there. He overturned the tables of the clerks and the stalls of those who were selling doves. He said to them, "It's written, 'My house will be called a house of prayer, but you've made it into a den of thieves.'"[3]

The blind and the disabled came to him in the temple, and he tended them. When the religious leaders and the lawyers saw the wonders he did and children in the temple area chanting, "Hosanna to the son of David," they were incensed.

"Do you hear what those children are saying?" they asked him.

"Yes," Jesus replied. "Have you ever read, 'From the lips of children and infants you have crafted perfect praise'?"

He left them and went away from the city to spend the night.[4]

In the morning, on the way back into the city, he was hungry. Seeing a fig tree at the side of the road, he went up to it but found only leaves. He said to it, "May you never again bear fruit." The tree dried up immediately.[5]

When his followers saw this, they were stunned. They asked, "How did that fig tree dry up so fast?"

Jesus said, "I've told you, if you trust and do not doubt, not only will you do what was done to this fig tree, but also you can tell the mountain, 'Rise up and drop into the sea,' and it will happen.

"If you only trust, you will get whatever you pray for."[6]

Jesus entered the temple and the religious leaders and elders approached him while he was teaching. They said, "Where do you get the authority to do these things? Who gave it to you?"

7 One well-recognized problem with formal religion is a tendency to talk about high-minded values without actually putting them into practice. But, then, we all do this. We profess high values and live with too much compromise. Jesus's utopian vision calls for a strong radical response.

8 This is a difficult lesson, especially for those who are used to thinking that being virtuous and always doing the right thing make you a good person. Jesus says that it is more likely that prostitutes will be in the kingdom than those who think of themselves as better than the rest. This is not just a challenge to churches but to each person who has the choice either to live as a member of the kingdom or to go through the motions and do it merely superficially.

Jesus replied, "Let me ask you a question. If you answer me, I'll tell you where I get the authority. Where did John's baptism come from? Was it from the heavens or was it human?"

They considered the question, thinking, "If we say it's from the heavens, he will say, 'Then why didn't you trust him?' But if we say it was human, we have to worry about the people. They think that John was a prophet."

They answered Jesus's question, "We don't know."

"Then I won't tell you where I get the authority for my actions.

"What is your opinion? A man had two sons. He approached the first one and said, 'Son, go to work today in my vineyard.'

"'No, I won't,' he said. But later he changed his mind and went.

"Then the father approached his other son and said the same thing. He responded, 'Yes, sir, I will.' But he didn't go.[7]

"Which of them did his father's will?"

"The first one," they said.

Jesus said to them, "I'm telling you, embezzlers and prostitutes will enter the kingdom of the sky before you do.[8] John came to show you an ethical way and you didn't trust him. But the embezzlers and prostitutes did. Even when you saw all this, you still didn't change your mind and trust him.

"Here's another parable. Listen. A landowner planted a vineyard. He built a wall around it, put a winepress in the ground, and set up a tower. Then he rented it to some farmers and went away on a trip. When it was time for the harvest, he sent servants to the tenants to collect his grapes.

"The tenants grabbed the servants. They beat up one, killed another, and stoned a third one. So he sent more servants, and

9   This is one of the constant building blocks of the kingdom: What is nor-
    mally rejected is here valued. This is also one of the deepest and most dif-
    ficult of psychological realizations: Whatever you reject might turn out to
    be the most valuable item of all.

10 Another slap at virtue. Those who believe themselves to be virtuous, good,
    and model people may say that they will follow the rules of the kingdom,
    but what counts is the fruit; that is, what you actually do. There is often a
    disparity between saying and doing. This is a deep issue: The illusion of vir-
    tue without follow-through leads to exclusion and disaster. Jesus would toss
    the dead wood into the fire.

the tenants treated them the same way. Finally, he sent his son. 'They'll show my son respect,' he thought.

"But when the tenants saw the son, they said to each other, 'He's the heir. Let's kill him and take the inheritance.' So they grabbed him, dragged him off the vineyard, and killed him.

"When the owner comes, what will he do to the tenants?"

"He'll kill the good-for-nothings," they said, "and he'll rent the vineyard to someone else, who will give him his share of the crops at the harvest."

Jesus said, "Did you ever read in the scriptures:

> *The stone the builders rejected*
> *Has become the cornerstone.*
> *The Master has done this*
> *And in our eyes it's wonderful.*[9]

"I can tell you now that the kingdom of God will be taken away from you and will be given to people who will produce fruit.[10]

"Whoever falls on this stone will be smashed to pieces, and whoever the stone falls on will be pulverized."

When the religious leaders and the Pharisees heard Jesus's parables, they knew he was talking about them. But they worried about the people, who considered him a prophet.

1   A rich image for the kingdom—a wedding party. Sacred marriage, *hieros gamos*, is a widespread and ancient image for the reconciliation of division and opposition within a person and within a society. A party also suggests the enjoyment of this life.

Theologian Mark C. Taylor puts it this way: "Jesus, one might say, was the first to declare the death of God. The incarnation of the divine in the human is the disappearance of transcendence in immanence" (Taylor). Taylor quotes Friedrich Nietzsche: "The Kingdom of God ... is an inward change in the individual, something that comes at every moment and at every moment has not yet arrived. Bliss is not something promised; it is there if you act in such and such a way" (Taylor).

2   What is this? You do not go to a wedding party and so your city is burned? It is a parable, a fiction with a point. We may be invited to live at a higher level, sublime *ouranic* values, but we decline. The result is disaster. It is worse for you if you decline than if you are not made aware of the possibility.

3   He was not dressed properly for the wedding so he is bound and thrown into darkness? Not only do you have to enter the kingdom, but you also have to be in every way a citizen of the kingdom. Show it. Dress like it. Really do it.

Chapter 22

Jesus spoke to them again in parables. "The kingdom is like a wedding party that a king created for his son.[1] He sent his staff to get the people he had invited, but they declined. Again he sent his representatives, saying, 'Tell those who were invited that I've prepared a dinner. My cattle and fattened animals have been butchered and everything is prepared. Come to the party.'

"But they ignored him and walked away. One went to his fields and another to his store. Others grabbed the servants, treated them badly, and even killed them. The king was outraged. He sent his army to deal with the murderers and set fire to their city.[2]

"Then he told his servants, 'The wedding party is ready, but the ones I invited don't deserve to come. Go out on the streets and invite anyone you see.' So the servants went out on the streets and gathered any people they could find, good and bad, and the wedding hall was filled with guests.

"But when the king came in to meet the guests, he saw a man who wasn't dressed for a wedding. 'My friend,' he said, 'how did you get in here without proper attire?' The man didn't know what to say.

"Then the king told the waiters, 'Tie him up, hands and feet, and throw him out into the darkness, where people will cry out and grit their teeth.'[3]

"Many are invited, but few have what it takes."

4   Many have seen the image of Socrates in Jesus the Teacher. David L. Miller
    explores this connection extensively in his book *Christs: Meditations on Arche-*
    typal Images in Christian Theology. He describes a passionate rather than overly
    intellectual Socrates: "Dionysian enthusiasm and eros give form to a teach-
    ing which cannot be distinguished from preaching. There is voice in the
    quiet whisperings of the inner soul, and there is soul in the crying out loud.
    Inner is outer, and outer has a deep interiority" (Miller).

Then the Pharisees went and made plans to trap him in his words. They enlisted some followers and associates of Herod. "Teacher," these people said, "we know that you're an honorable man and that you teach the word of God honestly.⁴ You aren't swayed by people, because you don't care who they are. So tell us, what do you think? Is it proper to pay taxes to Caesar or not?"

Knowing their malicious intentions, Jesus said, "You hypocrites. Why are you trying to trap me? Give me the coin used to pay the tax."

They gave him a denarius, and he asked them, "Whose picture is on this? Whose inscription?"

"Caesar's," they said.

Then he told them, "Give to Caesar what is Caesar's and to God what is God's."

When they heard this, they were impressed. So they let him go and went away.

That day, the Sadducees, who say that there is no resurrection, came to him with a query. "Teacher," they said, "Moses said that if a man dies without having children, his brother has to marry the widow and have children for him. We happen to know the story of seven brothers. The first got married and died. Since he didn't have any children, he left his wife to his brother. The same thing happened with the second and third brother, and right down to the seventh. Finally, the woman died. Of the seven, whose wife will she be at the resurrection? All of them were married to her."

Jesus answered, "No, that's not right. You don't understand the scriptures or God's ways. Those who have resurrected don't marry. They're like angels in the sky. As to the resurrection of the dead, have you ever read what God said? 'I am the God of

5   This key point could change the lives of many people who see religion
    mainly as having to do with the afterlife. Jesus speaks for a God of the living.

6   Psalm 110:1.

7   Here is Leo Tolstoy's version of this passage:

    > Christos is neither son of David, nor anyone's son after the flesh; but
    > Christos is that same lord, our Ruler, whom we know in ourselves
    > as our life. Christos is that understanding which is in us (Tolstoy).

    Christos is not a product of history alone but has a spiritual lineage, as we
    see thoroughly spelled out in the Book of John (Moore).

Abraham, the God of Isaac, and the God of Jacob.' He is not the God of the dead, but of the living."[5]

When the people heard this, they were impressed with his teaching.

Hearing that Jesus had made the Sadducees speechless, the Pharisees got together. One, a legal expert, tested him with this question. "Teacher, what is the most important requirement in the law?"

Jesus replied, "Love God, your Master, with your whole heart and soul and mind. This is the first and most important requirement. The second is similar: Love the other as you love yourself. The entire law and prophets depend on these two requirements."

When the Pharisees were together, Jesus asked them, "What do you think about the Christos? Whose son is he?"

They answered, "The son of David."

He said, "Then how can an inspired David call him master? Here's what he says:

> *The Master said to my Master,*
> *'Sit at my right hand*
> *until I put your enemies*
> *under your feet.'*[6]

"If David calls him 'Master,' how can he be his son?"[7]

No one could give him an answer, and from then on no one ventured to ask another question.

1   Perhaps this is a form of spiritual materialism discussed by Buddhist medita-
    tion master and scholar Chögyam Trungpa:

> "Ego can convert anything to its own use, even spirituality. Ego
> is constantly attempting to acquire and apply the teachings of
> spirituality for its own benefit ... The main point of any spiritual
> practice is to step out of the bureaucracy of ego. This means stepping
> out of ego's constant desire for a higher, more spiritual, more
> transcendental version of knowledge, religion, virtue, judgment,
> comfort, or whatever it is that the particular ego is seeking. One
> must step out of spiritual materialism" (Trungpa).

2   This mind-bending notion of authority sounds like Thomas Jefferson in the
    spirit of the American Revolution, only even more radical. This is a demo-
    cratic community. The point of leadership is to serve and not to be above
    anyone else. This passage must be an awesome challenge to hierarchies and
    authorities. It reveals the social restructuring in Jesus's vision—a radically
    egalitarian view of society. He has been hammering at this point all along.

Chapter 23

Then Jesus spoke to his followers and the people: "The law professors and the Pharisees take the place of Moses. You have to obey them, but you don't necessarily have to do what they do, because they don't themselves do what they teach. They put heavy burdens on people's shoulders, but they won't lift a finger to help.

"They do everything so people can see them.[1] They make their phylacteries big and their tassels long. They enjoy a place of honor at dinners and the best seats in the synagogues. They love signs of respect at the market. They want everyone to call them 'Rabbi.'

"You, on the other hand, should never be called 'Rabbi.' You have only one teacher. You are all brothers. Don't call anyone on earth 'father.' You have one father above. You shouldn't be called teacher either, because you have one teacher, Christos. The most important among you is a servant. Anyone who puts himself up high will be brought down, and anyone who is humble will be the highest of all.[2]

"Watch your step, you legalists and Pharisees. You're impostors. You keep people from entering the kingdom. You don't become part of it yourselves, and when others want to enter, you stand in their way. Watch out, you legalists and Pharisees. You'll go anywhere on sea or land to convert a single person and make him far more wicked and worldly than yourselves.

"Be careful, you blind overlords. You tell people that if they make vows in the temple their words don't mean anything, but if they make any promises having to do with the temple's

3   Once again, an emphasis on qualities of soul over formal rites and rules.

wealth, they're bound by them. You blind idiots. What is more important? The gold or the sanctuary that sanctifies the gold?

"You say, whoever makes a vow at the altar isn't bound by it, and yet whoever makes a vow secured by a donation at the altar is bound. How blind can you be? What is more important—the donation or the altar that sanctifies the donation?

"Anyone who makes a vow at the altar, vows by the altar and anything on it. Anyone who makes a vow in the temple, promises by the temple and anyone who abides there. Whoever makes a vow by the sky promises by God's very seat and by the one sitting there.

"Watch your step, you legalists and Pharisees. You require a tax on mint, dill, and cumin, and yet you overlook the really important issues of the law—ethics and kindness and trust. These are the things you should be concerned about, without entirely forgetting about the formal items.[3]

"You blind leaders. You filter out a gnat and swallow a camel.

"Watch out, you legalists and Pharisees. You disinfect the outside of the cup and plate, but the insides are still teeming with greed and self-interest. You blind Pharisees. You should clean the inside of the cup as well as the outside.

"Watch out, you legalists and Pharisees. You're like painted mausoleums. Outside they look great, but inside they're full of the bones of the dead and all sorts of filth. In the same way, on the outside you look beatific, but inside you're full of hypocrisy and scheming.

"Watch out, legalists and Pharisees. Pretenders. You build monuments to the prophets and you decorate the tombs of the good. You say, 'If we had been around in the days of the prophets, we wouldn't have had anything to do with shedding their blood.' But you betray yourselves, because you're the descendants of those who killed the prophets. Own up to it. You are

4   This Jerusalem is also our contemporary society that does not recognize higher values but continues to live from anxiety and self-interest. Jesus speaks for a higher set of values. Perhaps one day we will collectively understand that utopia is reachable and that the Jesus vision is what we have been looking for.

the descendants of those who killed the prophets. Admit what
your ancestors did.

"You snakes. You brood of vipers. How can you avoid being
thrown into Gehenna?

"I'm sending you prophets, wise and intelligent people. Some of
them you'll crucify and murder. Some of them you'll flog in your
synagogues and hunt down from city to city. All the precious
blood shed on the land will be on your heads, from the blood
of law-abiding Abel to that of Zechariah, son of Barachiah. You
murdered him somewhere between the sanctuary and the altar.
Eventually, it will all come down on this gang.

"Jerusalem, Jerusalem. A city that kills prophets and stones
those sent to it. Many times I have wanted to bring your children together like a hen gathering her brood under her wings,
but you didn't want me. Look, you're left empty. I warn you,
you won't see me again until you say, 'Let's celebrate this man
who comes in the name of the Lord.'"⁴

1   Remember that Jesus speaks in parables. Here he is saying the overorganized
    religion will topple. In its place will be a deeply personal and communal
    spiritual way of life, based on the many teachings offered in the Gospels.

2   "The verb *euangel-izesthai* [the root of 'gospel'] occurs for the first time in
    Greek literature in Aristophanes. It is used for bringing news about victories
    and other joyful events, but soon becomes synonymous with and stands for
    the bringing of any news, good or bad…. By the middle of the [second]
    century CE some proof for the use of the term 'gospel' as a designation of
    written documents begins to appear."
       —Helmut Koester, *Ancient Christosian Gospels: Their History and Development*
       (Harrisburg, PA: Trinity Press International, 1990), 1, 17

3   My dream of April 10, 2010: I am eating alone. Everyone is going to the
    airport. I go along, hoping to get home. I am in a hotel to await the plane
    overnight. I have forgotten my things back at the house. I am told not to go
    back for them. At the airport, an attendant tells me to look on a blackboard
    for time of departure. The blackboard is blank. She says, "Be ready now." It
    is 7 p.m. now and I know that the plane will take off at 3 a.m.
       Another person's dream in June 2011: He is in a car that comes to a stop.
    A nice woman invites him to a dinner honoring his and his wife's sixtieth
    wedding anniversary. He knows that the anniversary is still two years off. He
    wants to ignore the smiling woman's plans, but maybe he should not.
       These dreams suggest an archetypal quality to Jesus's theme of being pre-
    pared. Do what you can now, even if it seems too early, to be in the king-
    dom. Do not wait. The kingdom is available at this very moment, not later.

Chapter 24

Jesus walked away from the temple, and his followers drew his attention to the buildings.

He said, "You see all this? I warn you, not one stone will remain on top of another. The whole thing will be toppled."[1]

When he was sitting down at the Mount of Olives, his followers approached him privately and said, "Tell us when all this will happen. What will we see as a sign that you have arrived? What will be the signal that the current era has ended?"

Jesus said, "Be careful. Don't let anyone mislead you. Many will appear using my name and say, 'I'm the messiah.' In fact, they'll mislead many. You'll hear of warfare and rumors of warfare. Don't be upset. This has to happen, but the end is not here yet. Country will arm against country, nation against nation. There will be famines and earthquakes everywhere. This is just the start of the birth pangs.

"They'll turn you in to be tortured and you will be killed. Because of your connection with my name, every group will detest you. Many will drift away. They'll hate and betray each other. Many false prophets will appear and mislead people. Terrible events will take place and people will become depressed. The patient ones will survive. This Gospel[2] will be spoken to people throughout the world, and then the end will appear.

"When you notice dishonor replacing holiness, as the Prophet Daniel put it, if you're in Judea, you should escape to the mountains. If you're on your rooftop, don't go down into the house for your belongings. If you're in a field, don't go to your house to get a coat.[3]

4   "The glory is the presence, not the essence of God; an act rather than a qual-
    ity; a process not a substance.... The glory reflects abundance of good and
    truth, the power that acts in nature and history.... The outwardness of the
    world communicates something of the indwelling greatness of God, which
    is radiant and conveys itself without words."
        —Abraham J. Heschel, *Between God and Man: An Interpretation of Judaism* (New
        York: Simon and Schuster, 1959), 56

5   If you take all the strong apocalyptic language poetically, you can see how it
    signals a major shift in the way a society or an individual handles change in
    the face of disturbance or disaster. Jesus recommends again and again paying
    attention to all indications of change and being prepared. If you see signs of
    disruption in your life, like a failed career or marriage, get ready for a deep,
    spiritual shift. A world is coming to an end.

"Pity those who are pregnant or nursing then and pray that your escape won't be in winter or on the Sabbath. There will be enormous suffering then, a kind never before seen from the beginning of creation—and there will never be anything like it again. If this period were not so brief, no one would survive. But for the sake of the chosen, it will be short.

"If someone says, 'Here's Christos' or 'There he is,' don't believe it. Pseudo-Christos and pseudo-prophets will appear and produce incredible signs and omens and will mislead even the chosen. Remember, I told you.

"If they say, 'Hey, he's out in the wilderness,' don't go out there. If they say, 'He's in the private rooms,' don't trust them. The son of man will appear like lightning rising in the east and flashing in the west. Where the body lies, that's where the vultures will gather.

> "*Right after these times of torment,*
> *the sun will go dark*
> *and the moon will fail to shine,*
> *the stars will fall out of the sky*
> *and the graceful cycle of planets*
> *will finally and completely fail.*

"Then the sign of the son of man will appear in the sky and all the nations on earth will be astonished. They'll see the son of man with stunning force and glory arriving on clouds.⁴ With a loud trumpet blast he'll dispatch his angels and they will collect the chosen from the four winds and across the sky.⁵

6   I love Jesus,
     Who told us:
     Heaven and Earth will go
     When heaven and earth go
     My word will stay.
     Your word? Which word, Jesus?
     Love, forgiveness, charity?
     All your words are really one:
     Stay awake.
       —Antonio Machado [translation mine]

7   You have to be alert and quick-witted to be in the kingdom. Unconscious-
    ness drags you down and puts you to sleep. You tarry and procrastinate.
    The culture around you wants to absorb you, swallow you up. Jesus always
    recommends readiness.

"Learn this lesson from the fig tree: When its branches grow soft and its leaves appear, you know that summer is near. So, when you see all these things, know that he is near, ready at the gates. I assure you that this era will not pass away until all of this happens. Earth and sky will pass, but my words won't.

"No one knows the hour or the day—not the messengers, not the son, but the father alone. As it was for Noah, so for the son of man. Minutes before the flood, people were eating and drinking, marrying and giving in marriage, until the very day that Noah got into the ark. They knew nothing until the flood came and swept them all away. This is how the son of man will come, too.

"Two will be in the field. One will be taken and one left behind. Two women will be grinding grain together. One will be taken and one left behind. So stay awake. You don't know the day or the hour your master is coming.⁶

"Know this: If the owner of the house knew just when the thief would appear, he'd stay awake and wouldn't let his house be broken into. You have to be ready. The son of man is coming at an hour completely unexpected.

"Who is the wise and able servant the master put in charge of the house? He'll give the other servants the right food at the right time. Lucky is the servant the master finds at work when he arrives. To be sure, he'll put him in charge of everything.

"But if the servant is wicked and thinks, 'My master will be late,' and starts beating his fellow servants and eats and drinks with drunks, the master will arrive on a day when he's not expected and at an unforeseen hour. He will cut him off and put him in with the hypocrites, where there will be anguish and pain."⁷

1   In a sense, you enter the kingdom every minute of your life, yet it is easy to fall back into unconsciousness. You have to be alert at all times. You always have the opportunity to let the old way fall apart and once again try the new. If you are not prepared, you may well succumb to the old way.

Chapter 25

"The kingdom is like ten virgins who took their torches and went out to greet the groom. Five were foolish and five wise. The foolish ones brought their torches but no extra oil. The wise brought oil in jars for the torches. The groom was delayed for a long time and they became drowsy and fell asleep. Then at midnight a cry went up: 'The groom is here. Come greet him.'

"All the virgins woke up and got their torches ready. The foolish ones said to the wise ones, 'Share your oil. Our torches are out.'

"'No,' they said. 'There's not enough for us all. Better to go to the oil shop and buy some yourselves.' But while they were gone, the groom showed up. The alert virgins joined the party with him and the door closed. The others arrived in due time. 'Sir, sir,' they said, 'open the door for us.'

"He said, 'Do I know you?'

"Stay alert, because you don't know the day or the hour.[1]

"Similarly, a person went on a long trip. He summoned his employees and secured his things with them. He gave one five thousand dollars, and another two and another one, according to each person's qualifications. Then he went on his trip.

"The one who had received five thousand put his money to work and acquired five thousand more. The one with two thousand gained two. But the person who had received one thousand went off and buried it.

"A while later the master returned to settle accounts. The one who had received five thousand dollars brought the additional

2   "The conservative servant had correctly seen that life is full of risks, but he drew the wrong conclusion. Seeing the risk of losing, he was reluctant to make any investment. The correct logic is that since life is full of hazards regardless of what we do, we should be more adventurous."
    —Kenneth S. Leong, *The Zen Teachings of Jesus* (New York: Crossroad, 2001), 110

3   A key spiritual problem in modern life is everyday unconsciousness. People just accept that life is about making money and being comfortable. Then they suffer depressions and loss of purpose and wonder why. Alongside unconsciousness is the failure to tend the spirit and soul. Unconsciousness and deep-seated passivity make for lost lives. Jesus's main mission is to counter this tendency and to show what it is like to really be alive.

five thousand and said, 'Master, you trusted me with five thousand dollars and I've made five thousand more.'

"The master said, 'Well done. You're a good and loyal servant. You've been trustworthy with a few things, so I'll put you in charge of more. Come and celebrate with me.'

"The man who had received two thousand showed up. 'Master,' he said, 'you trusted me with two thousand and I've acquired two thousand more.'

"The master replied, 'Well done. You're a good and loyal servant. You've been trustworthy with a few things, so I'll put you in charge of more. Come and celebrate with me.'

"Then the person with one thousand dollars came. 'Master,' he said, 'I knew you to be a harsh man. You gather up grain where you haven't planted it. I was afraid. I went out and buried your money in the ground. Here, this is yours.'

"The master replied, 'You wicked, lazy employee. You knew that I harvest grain where I haven't planted it? Then you should have deposited the money with bankers. When I got back, I could have had it with interest.'[2]

"Take the money from him and give it to the one with the ten thousand. Anyone who has something will get more and have plenty. Whoever has nothing will lose what he has. Toss this wicked servant out into the dark where there will be pain and agony.[3]

4   Here we see an important connection between how we live every day and
    our spiritual condition. What we do in our secular lives affects our spirit and
    makes all the difference in who we are at a deep and meaningful level. The
    longing for a sense of purpose is widespread and deeply felt, but it often
    appears to be something to do rather than someone to be.

"When the son of man comes in all his sparkle and his angels with him, he will sit on his throne of grace. The people of the world gather in front of him, and he will divide them up as a shepherd separates sheep from goats. He will put sheep on the right and goats on the left.

"Then the king will say to those on his right, 'Come. My father has blessed you. Inherit the kingdom that was being prepared for you ever since the world was conceived.'

> *"I was hungry and you gave me food.*
> *"I was thirsty and you gave me drink.*
> *"I was a stranger and you took me in.*
> *"I was naked and you dressed me.*
> *"I was sick and you tended me.*
> *"I was in prison and you visited me.*

"Then those with honor will answer him,

> *"'Sir, when did we notice your hunger and feed you?*
> *"'When did we notice your thirst and give you drink?*
> *"'When did we notice that you were a stranger and take you in?*
> *"'When did we notice that you were naked and dress you?*
> *"'When did we notice that you were sick or in prison and visit you?'*

"The king will answer, 'You should know that whatever you have done for the most insignificant of my brothers, you have done for me.'⁴

5   This passage encourages us to see Jesus as an archetypal figure, a model, educating and feeding our imagination as we deal with the world in which we live. As he says, he is the way. He embodies the teaching, indeed the kingdom itself. So to treat people well is to treat him and his teaching well. You honor him by living his values.

6   "Eternal" here does not have to refer to the afterlife. It means timeless, profound, essential; a matter of soul and spirit. If you take care of the world and its people, you will have a profound feeling of being alive, in your spirit and soul as well as your body.

"Then he will speak to those on his left. 'Get out, you're cursed. Go to the eternal fire created for the devil and his angels.'

> *"I was hungry, and you gave me nothing to eat.*
> *"I was thirsty, and you gave me nothing to drink.*
> *"I was a stranger, and you didn't take me in.*
> *"I was in need of clothing and you didn't dress me.*
> *"I was sick and in prison and you didn't look after me.*

"They will respond. 'Sir, when did we see you hungry or thirsty or a stranger or in need of clothes or sick or in prison and didn't help?'

"He will answer, 'Whatever you failed to do for the least of these people, you failed to do for me.'[5]

"Then they will go to eternal punishment and the good ones to eternal life."[6]

1   "... [T]he anointing was not a haphazard, spur-of-the-moment action by a
sobbing sinner, ... but was a pre-arranged sacred ritual, the purpose of which
was not known to the twelve men."
    —Lynn Picknett, *Mary Magdalene* (London: Robinson, 2003), 55

2   This story has many levels. Jesus is Christos, the man of oil. His anointing signifies the basic idea of his kingdom: raising human life to a level far
beyond or above unconscious greed and self-absorption. The kingdom is
an intensification of life. Further, it is not part of the typical male system of
culture, characterized by conquest and violence. A woman anoints Jesus,
giving him the simple pleasure of an oil rub. The Greek Aphrodite lies in the
background. The male order gives way to a mixed-gender way of life.

Chapter 26

When Jesus finished saying these things, he addressed his students: "Do you realize that the Passover will be here in two days? They'll arrest and crucify the son of man."

The religious leaders and elders among the people gathered in the courtyard of the chief priest, Caiaphas. They schemed how to arrest Jesus and kill him. "But not during the festival," they warned, "or the people could riot."

Jesus was in Bethany in the home of Simon the Leper, when a woman approached him with an alabaster jar full of expensive oils and poured a few drops on his head as he was sitting at the table.[1]

When his companions noticed this, they were upset. "What a waste," they said. "This perfume could have been sold at a good price and the money given to the poor."

Jesus heard what they said. "Why are you complaining about this woman? She did a beautiful thing. You'll always have the poor around, but you won't always have me. When she poured oil on my body she was preparing me for burial. I assure you, wherever in the world people read this Gospel, they'll hear about what she did."[2]

3 A festival commemorating the Exodus from Egypt during which the people could not bake leavened bread. It is connected to the Passover festival.

Then one of the twelve, Judas Iscariot, left and talked with the chief priests. "If I betray Jesus to you, what's in it for me?" They figured thirty silver coins would do it. From that moment on Judas looked for an opportunity.

On the first day of the Unleavened Bread,[3] his followers asked Jesus, "Where would you like us to prepare the Passover meal?"

He said, "Go to that fellow in the city and tell him, 'The teacher says that the moment we've been waiting for has come. I'll celebrate the Passover with my friends at your house.'"

His students did what he said and prepared for Passover.

When evening came, Jesus reclined at the table with the twelve. As they were eating, he said, "I should probably tell you. One of you is going to betray me."

They were upset and said to him, one after another, "Not I, sir?"

Jesus answered, "Someone who has dipped his fingers into the bowl with me will betray me. The son of man will go through exactly what was written about him. But pity the person who betrays him. It would be better if he had never been born."

Then Judas, the would-be betrayer, said, "It can't be me."

Jesus said, "But you've spoken."

4   A crucial passage. Jesus's blood, equal to wine, a substance that transforms
    and intoxicates in a spiritual, Dionysian sense, will have a different kind of
    reality, as does everything else, in the kingdom of the Sky Father. The spiri-
    tuality that is coming will be a rapturous one.

5   This whole section from the Last Supper to the Mount of Olives is intense in
    the text, and spare. I am here letting the language break apart, tend toward
    the poetic, as it does somewhat in the original.

6   The Greek word for "eager" here is an interesting one: *prothymos. Thymos* is a
    word for "soul" or "passion." The modern manual of psychological disorders
    lists dysthymia, a failure of *thymos*, and describes it as a kind of depression.

While they were eating, Jesus picked up bread and blessed it and broke it and gave it to his students and said, "Pick it up and eat it. This is my body."

He put the cup in his hands, offered thanks, and gave it to them, saying, "Everyone, drink from it. This is my blood, my last will, poured out for many, as forgiveness for their bad actions. I can tell you that I won't drink this fruit of the vine until the day when I drink a new wine with you in my father's kingdom."4

They sang a hymn and then went to the Mount of Olives.

Jesus told them, "Tonight you will be less sure of me. The scriptures say, 'I will threaten the shepherd and the flock will scatter.'

"But after I wake up I will go ahead of you into Galilee."

Peter said, "I don't care if everyone loses faith in you. I never will."

"I assure you," Jesus replied. "Tonight, before the rooster crows, three times you will deny any connection with me."

Peter said, "Even if I must die with you, I will never renounce you." All of them said the same.

Then Jesus went with them to a place called Gethsemane and said to them, "Stay here while I go off to pray." He took Peter and the two sons of Zebedee with him. He felt depressed and troubled and told them, "My soul is deeply distressed, to the very death. Stay with me and keep alert."

Going a short distance further he bent over with his face to the ground and prayed, "My father, if it is at all possible, spare me this cup, yet what I want is not important; it's what you desire."5

He went back to his followers and found them asleep. He said to Peter, "Couldn't you stay awake with me for one hour? Be very careful. Don't get into a situation where you will be tested. The spirit is eager but the body isn't so strong."6

7   No time ago
    or else a life
    walking in the dark
    i met christ

    jesus) my heart
    flopped over
    and lay still
    while he passed (as

    close as I'm to you
    yes closer
    made of nothing
    except loneliness.
        —E. E. Cummings, *Complete Poems 1904–1962*, edited by George J. Firmage
        (New York: Liveright, 1991), 648

8   "If someone should happen to find himself in a situation where he recognizes
    an imminent danger that he will be driven by force to offend God, he ought
    to do what the apostles did—avoid capture by fleeing."
        —Thomas More, *St. Thomas More: Selected Writing*, edited by John F. Thornton
        and Susan B. Varenne (New York: Vintage Books, 2003), 110

    We have to use every strategy we can imagine to avoid living the values of
    the old, corrupt world.

He went off a second time and prayed, "If I can't be spared this cup, if I have to drink it, then let your plan proceed."

When he returned, he found them asleep again. Their eyes were heavy. So he left them there and went off a third time and prayed in the same way.[7]

Finally, he returned to his companions once again. "Are you still asleep? Look around, the time is drawing near. The son of man is being betrayed. He is now in the hands of the ignorant. Get up now. Let's go. They come. My betrayer."

As he was speaking, one of the twelve, Judas, arrived. He came with a large crowd carrying swords and clubs. The chief priests and elders among the people had sent them. Earlier, the betrayer had arranged a signal for them. "The person I kiss is the one. Take him." Going up to Jesus right away, Judas said, "Hello, Rabbi," and kissed him tenderly.

Jesus said, "So you've come. Do it."

Men stepped forward, grabbed Jesus, and took him away. Then someone who was with Jesus reached for his sword, took it out, and struck a servant of the high priest and sliced off his ear.

"Put your sword back," Jesus said. "Whoever lives by a sword will die by a sword.

"Don't you understand that I could call on my father and he would send a hundred thousand angels to help me? But then how could the scriptures be fulfilled? It has to happen this way."

Then Jesus spoke to the crowd. "Have you come out with swords and sticks to arrest me, as though I were a criminal? I sat in the temple every day, and you didn't do anything to me. No, all this is taking place to fulfill the words of the prophets."

Then all his companions abandoned him and ran off.[8]

9   In Jesus's response to the high priest, once again we find a reference to the sky. He has been saying all along that he represents a point of view and a vision of the future that is not entirely worldly, and certainly not about worldly power. He speaks of a sky politics and power, one that is spiritual, idealistic, and utopian. We need this sky vision or else we will be locked in the prison of our pragmatic and neurotic ways. Earth and sky are the two parallel metaphors, and Jesus speaks for the sky.

They took him to the high priest, Caiaphas, where lawyers and elders had assembled. Peter followed at a distance. He stood in the courtyard of the high priest, then he went in and sat down with the guards to see what would happen.

Many people came forward and committed perjury. The chief priests and the entire Sanhedrin, the council of Jerusalem, were expecting fraudulent witnesses against Jesus so they could sentence him to death. But they didn't find what they were looking for.

But then two more witnesses came forward. This man said, "I can destroy the temple of God and rebuild it in three days."

The high priest rose and said, "What is this charge that these men have brought against you? Do you have a response?"

Jesus kept quiet.

The high priest said to him, "I demand that you swear by the living God and tell us if you are the Christos, the son of God."

Jesus said to him, "You are the one speaking, but let me say something to you.

> *"One day you will see the son of man*
> *Seated at the right hand of powerful forces*
> *Arriving on clouds in the sky."*[9]

Then the high priest ripped his clothes and said, "Blasphemy! He has spoken blasphemy. Do we need any more testimony? See, you've heard the blasphemy. What's your decision?"

"Death," they said. "He deserves death."

Then they spit in his face and beat him with their fists. Some slapped him and said, "Prophesy for us, Christos. Who hit you?"

10 This story of Peter's betrayal has moved readers for centuries. It is consistent with the Gospel approach: Imperfect people who feel remorse and change are good candidates for the kingdom, better than those who think they are perfect. Peter, the remorseful betrayer, assumes leadership, along with Mary of Magdalene and the "Beloved Disciple."

Peter was sitting out in the courtyard and a servant girl came up to him. "You were there with Jesus of Galilee," she said.

But in front of them all he exclaimed, "No, I don't know what you're talking about."

He went to the gate and another young woman saw him and told the people there, "This fellow was with Jesus of Nazareth."

Again he denied it and swore. "I don't even know the man."

After a while, some people standing there approached Peter and said, "Surely, you're one of them. Your accent says it all."

He called down curses on himself and swore to them, "I don't know the man."

Suddenly a rooster crowed.

Peter recalled what Jesus had said, "Before the rooster crows, you'll disown me three times." He left and wept bitterly.[10]

1   Jeremiah 32:6–10.

Chapter 27

In the morning all the chief priests and elders deliberated about putting Jesus to death. They tied him up, led him out, and handed him over to the governor, Pilate.

When Judas, the betrayer, saw that Jesus had been condemned, he felt a change come over him and returned the thirty silver coins to the chief priests and the elders, saying, "I have made a terrible mistake. I have betrayed innocent blood."

"What does that have to do with us?" they said. "That's your business."

Judas tossed the silver coins into the temple and left. He went off and hanged himself.

The chief priests picked up the coins and said, "It isn't legal to put this into the treasury, since it's blood money." They decided to use the money to buy a potter's field for burying foreigners. For that reason, it has been called the Field of Blood to this day and Jeremiah's words were fulfilled:

> *They used the thirty silver coins,*
> *The price placed on him by the people of Israel,*
> *To purchase a potter's field,*
> *Just as the master had instructed.* [1]

2   "Whenever the Divine appears in all Its depth, It cannot be endured by men.
     It must be pushed away by the political powers, the religious authorities, and
     the bearers of cultural tradition. In the picture of the Crucified, we look at
     the rejection of the Divine by humanity.... Whenever the Divine manifests
     Itself as the new reality, It must be rejected by the representatives of the old
     reality."
          —Paul Tillich, "He Who Is the Christos," in *The Shaking of the Foundations* (New
          York: Charles Scribner's Sons, 1948), 147

In the meantime, Jesus stood before the governor, who asked him, "Are you king of the Jews?"

"Whatever you say," Jesus said.

When the chief priests and elders accused him, he didn't respond.

Then Pilate said, "Have you heard the witnesses speaking against you?"

Jesus didn't respond to any of the charges. The governor was dismayed.

It was customary at the festival for the governor to release a prisoner that the people would choose. At that time they had an infamous character named Barabbas. When the crowd formed, Pilate asked them, "Who do you want me to free, Barabbas or Jesus, called Christos?" He knew that they had brought Jesus to him out of envy.

Pilate was sitting at the judge's bench, when his wife sent him a message: "Don't have anything to do with that good man. I have felt terrible all day because of a dream I had about him."

But the chief priests and elders convinced the people to ask for Barabbas and to execute Jesus.

"Which of these two do you want me to free?" asked the governor.

"Barabbas," they said.

"What should I do with Jesus, who is called Christos?" Pilate asked.

They all responded, "The cross!"

When Pilate realized that he could do nothing and that unrest was increasing, he asked for some water and washed his hands before the mob. "I am innocent of this man's blood," he said. "It's up to you now."

All the people shouted, "Let his blood be on us and our children."[2]

3   "Paradise was the navel of the Earth and ... Adam was created at the center
    of the earth, at the same spot where the Cross of Christos was later to be
    set up. The Jewish apocalypse and a midrash state that Adam was formed in
    Jerusalem. Adam being buried at the very spot where he was created, i.e., at
    the center of the world, on Golgotha, the blood of the Saviour will redeem
    him too."
        —Mircea Eliade, *The Myth of the Eternal Return*, translated by Willard R. Trask
        (Princeton, NJ: Princeton University Press, 1974), 16–17

4   These observers, of course, see the situation entirely the wrong way. Jesus is
    giving in to his destiny, the cross. He cannot come off it. He cannot expect
    deliverance. He has to go through what has been ordained for him. It is the
    same with all of us. We have to live the life given to us. We cannot expect a
    miracle to save us from ourselves. We all have to embrace our tragedies.

He freed Barabbas but had Jesus flogged and signed him over for crucifixion.

The governor's soldiers brought Jesus into the Praetorium, the headquarters hall, where a squadron of soldiers surrounded him. They stripped him and dressed him in a scarlet robe. They weaved thorns together into a crown and placed it on his head and put a reed in his right hand and bowed before him mockingly. "Hail, King of the Jews," they said. They spit on him and took the reed and hit him on the head repeatedly. After taunting him, they pulled off the robe and dressed him in his own clothes. Then they led him off for crucifixion.

As they were leaving, they ran into a man from Cyrene named Simon, whom they compelled to carry the cross. They arrived at the place known as Golgotha (Place of the Skull). For a drink they gave him sour wine mixed with bitters, but when he tasted it, he wouldn't drink it.[3]

After they crucified him, they divided up his clothes by throwing dice. Then they sat down and kept watch over him. Over his head they attached a written notice of his crime: "This Is Jesus, King of the Jews."

Two thieves were crucified with him, one on his right and one on his left. Passersby shook their heads and sneered at him, saying, "You're the one who was going to tear down the temple and rebuild it in three days? Save yourself. If you're a son of God, get down from the cross."

The chief priests, lawyers, and elders also derided him. "He saved others," they said, "but he can't save himself. He's the king of Israel? Then let's see him come down off that cross.[4] Then we'll have faith in him. If he trusts in God, let God save him now, if he wishes. He did say, 'I am a son of God.'"

The thieves crucified with him also insulted him.

5   "Christos crucified is the 'true Orpheus,' who carried home mankind as his
     bride from the depths of dark Hades."
         —Hugo Rahner, "The Christosian Mystery and the Pagan Mysteries," in
         The Mysteries: Papers from the Eranos Yearbooks, edited by Joseph Campbell
         (Princeton, NJ: Princeton University Press, 1955), 379

In these dark end pages of the Book of Matthew we see Jesus in the underworld of his destiny, going through all the torment to bring us out of our
particular darkness, the way the great singer Orpheus tried to rescue his
wife, Euridyce. Orpheus has been honored as a special figure who had the
ability to go into the Underworld and back for the benefit of humanity. In
tradition Jesus is the new Orpheus who dies for the benefit of humankind.

6   "Nowhere in the texts is there any indication that Christos regarded the
     women's contribution as inferior or subsidiary to that of his male disciples ...
     Unlike the eleven male disciples who feared for their own lives, the women
     disciples followed, were present at the crucifixion, witnessed the burial, dis-
     covered the empty tomb and, as true disciples, were rewarded with the first
     news of the resurrection and, in the case of Mary Magdalen, the first meet-
     ing with the risen Christos."
         —Susan Haskins, *Mary Magdalen: Myth and Metaphor* (New York: Riverhead
         Books, 1993), 11

From noon to three o'clock, darkness cast a shroud over the whole area. At about three o'clock, Jesus cried out loudly: *"Eloi, Eloi, lama sabachthani?"* That means, "My God, my God. Why have you abandoned me?"

Some of those standing there heard this and said, "He's calling for Elijah."

Quickly one of them ran and soaked a sponge in sour wine, put it on a pole, and offered it to Jesus to drink.

The others said, "Leave him be. Let's see if Elijah comes to help him."

Jesus cried out again loudly and his spirit departed.[5]

At that moment the temple's veils were torn in two from top to bottom. The earth shook and rocks split. Tombs opened up and bodies of the blessed that had passed on got up. They left their tombs behind and after Jesus's rising went to the holy city and appeared to many people.

When the centurion and his companions guarding Jesus saw the earthquake and everything that took place, they were terrified and said, "He must have been a son of God."

Several women were also present, watching at a distance. They had followed Jesus from Galilee, taking care of him. Among them were Mary of Magdala, Mary the mother of James and Joses, and the mother of Zebedee's sons.[6]

At evening time, Joseph, a wealthy man from Arimathea, arrived. He, too, was a follower of Jesus. He requested Jesus's body from Pilate and the governor ordered that the body be given to him. Joseph retrieved the body, wrapped it in a clean linen cloth, and placed it in his own new tomb that he had cut out of rock. He rolled a large stone in front of the entrance of

7   Once again, take this story about securing Jesus's body as a story, not as his-
    tory. Or think of it as having theological and even psychological meaning.
    The Gospels invite us to live the life Jesus models, including resurrecting—
    not literally from death, but spiritually, from being soul-dead. There is an
    urge in us, like the urge of the priests and Pilate, that would like to keep this
    resurrection from happening. We put big rocks against being wakened into a
    new vision and a new way of being.

the tomb and left. Mary of Magdala and the other Mary sat across from the tomb.

The day after Preparation Day, the chief priests and the Pharisees approached Pilate. "Sir, we recall that when he was alive the tramp said, 'In three days I will wake up.' Maybe you should give instructions that the tomb be made secure until the third day. It's possible that his followers might come and take the body and tell people that he woke up from death. This final deception would be more of a problem than the first."

"Go and make the tomb as secure as you can," Pilate said. So they went and secured the tomb, sealing the rock and posting a sentry.[7]

1   "When we say Jesus has risen from the dead, we do not mean that his corpse
was resuscitated and that he came back to the same kind of life as we know
it; that, after all, would be only a return to impermanence and an orien-
tation to death.... Jesus has entered into a new and permanent manner of
existence—immortal, deathless, no longer limited by our categories of space
and time."

> —Donald Spoto, *The Hidden Jesus: A New Life* (New York: St. Martin's Press,
> 1998), 236, 246

We all are resurrected when we "get up" from the darkness and stupor of our
unconsciousness and acting-out. We live an entirely new kind of existence.

Chapter 28

After the Sabbath, at dawn on the first day of the week, Mary of Magdala and the other Mary inspected the tomb. Suddenly the earth shook and an angel of the Lord came down from the sky. He went over to the tomb and rolled back the rock and sat on it. He looked like lightning. His clothes were absolutely white, like snow. The guards were so terrified that they trembled and looked like death.

The angel said to the women, "Don't be afraid. I'm aware that you are looking for Jesus, who was crucified. He is not here. Just as he said, he has risen. Come and look at the place where he lay. Then quickly go and inform his followers. He woke up from death and will arrive in Galilee ahead of you. You'll see him there. Remember what I'm telling you."¹ The women rushed away from the tomb, full of fear and yet joyful as well, and hurried to inform the students.

Jesus approached them. "Hello," he said. They came to him and caressed his feet and showed him great honor. Jesus said, "Don't be afraid. Go, tell my brothers to travel to Galilee and we'll see each other there."

Once the women had gone, the guards went to the city and reported everything to the chief priests. They met with the elders and came up with a plan. They gave the soldiers a lot of money and told them to say that during the night his followers came and took him when they were asleep: "If the governor hears about it, we'll deal with him and keep you out of trouble."

The soldiers took the money and did as they were told. To this very day, this story makes its rounds among Jews.

2 Jesus lives in his vision for humanity, and it is a vision for the whole world, not for a chosen few. It includes earth and sky, metaphors for ordinary life quickened by utopian sky values. The passage ends beautifully with the comforting blessing that the Jesus way will be possible for us forever. He is with us in his vision, his philosophy that counters worldly wisdom and practice. We need not give up our idealism and optimism. It is possible to achieve the beautiful communal way of life that Jesus teaches, a life rooted in mutual respect, all-around forgiveness, and deep friendship.

Then the eleven disciples went to Galilee, to the mountain Jesus had mentioned. When they saw him, they treated him with great respect, and yet some were doubtful. Jesus said to them, "I have been given complete power on earth and in the sky. So, go. Make all countries followers. Baptize them in the name of the father, the son, and the holy spirit. Show them how to observe everything I've taught you. Never forget that I am always with you, to the very end of time."[2]

Acknowledgments

I took on this project with a strong desire to make a contribution but sharply aware of my limitations. So I am especially grateful for the support and ideas of old friends and new colleagues. In this case I want to make the usual disclaimer: In thanking the following accomplished men and women I do not want to imply that my work reflects their opinions. In all cases there would probably be some essential disagreements. Still, thank you to the old friends Jean Lall, Alice O. Howell, Christopher Bamford, Pat Toomay, George Nickelsburg, John Dominic Crossan, Rev. Marcus McKinney, Ruth Rusca, Timothy Freke, Patrice Pinette, and especially Hari Kirin Khalsa, and to the thoughtful people at Sky-Light Paths Publishing, especially Emily Wichland and Leah Brewer.

Notes

Introduction to Gospel

1. Translations and writings on the Gospels often include chapter and verse when passages are cited. I do not include the verse because I want the reader to have a fresh, clear experience of the text. I hope that the absence of verse numbers will intensify the feeling of reading poetry, rather than prose, for study. This means that it may be slightly more difficult to navigate the text, but I think the emphasis on the poetic is more important.

2. John G. Neihardt, *Black Elk Speaks* (New York: Pocket Books, 1959), 25.

Introduction to the Book of Matthew

1. Oscar Wilde, *De Profundis* (New York: Modern Library, 2000).

Chapter 3

10. C. G. Jung, *Symbols of Transformation*, translated by R.F.C. Hull (Princeton, NJ: Princeton University Press, 1967), 198.

Chapter 4

1. C. G. Jung, *Psychology and Religion*, translated by R.F.C. Hull (Princeton, NJ: Princeton University Press, 1969), 385.

Chapter 5

3. Ernest Jones, C. G. Jung, and James Hillman, *Salt and the Alchemical Soul* (Woodstock, CT: Spring Publications, 1995), 171.

Chapter 8

4. Robert Funk, *Jesus as Precursor* (Missoula, MT: Society of Biblical Literature, 1975), 101; and Thomas Merton, *Conjectures of a Guilty Bystander* (New York: Doubleday, 1989), 249.

Chapter 9

2. Michael Grant, *Jesus* (London: Weidenfeld and Nicolson, 1977), 113.

Chapter 12

5. Rollo May, *Love and Will* (New York: W.W. Norton, 1969), 123.

Chapter 13

10. Bernard Brandon Scott, *Re-Imagine the World: An Introduction to the Parables of Jesus* (Santa Rosa, CA: Polebridge Press, 2001), 34.

Chapter 17

4. Walter Burkert, *Greek Religion*, translated by John Raffan (Cambridge, MA: Harvard University Press, 1985), 180.

Chapter 19

4. Shunryu Suzuki, *Zen Mind, Beginner's Mind* (New York: Weatherhill, 1994), 44.

Chapter 20

3. Lao Tzu, *Tao Te Ching*, translated by Gia-Fu Feng and Jane English (New York: Vintage, 1972), 63.

4. Ibid., 66.

Chapter 22

1. Mark C. Taylor, *Nots* (Chicago: University of Chicago Press, 1993), 60.

4. David L. Miller, *Christs: Meditations on Archetypal Images in Christian Theology* (New York: Seabury Press, 1981), 125.

7. Leo Tolstoy, *The Gospel in Brief* (Lincoln: University of Nebraska Press, 2008), 172; and Thomas Moore, *Gospel—The Book of John: A New Translation with Commentary* (Woodstock, VT: SkyLight Paths, forthcoming).

Chapter 23

1. Chögyam Trungpa, *Cutting Through Spiritual Materialism* (Boston: Shambhala, 1987), 13, 15.

Suggestions for Further Reading

Borg, Marcus, ed. *Jesus at 2000*. Boulder, CO: Westview Press, 1998.

Crossan, John Dominic. *Jesus: A Revolutionary Biography*. San Francisco: HarperOne, 2009.

Fideler, David. *Jesus Christ, Sun of God: Ancient Cosmology and Early Christian Symbolism*. Wheaton, IL: Quest Books, 1993.

Funk, Robert. *Jesus as Precursor*. Sonoma, CA: Polebridge Press, 1994.

Haskins, Susan. *Mary Magdalen: Myth and Metaphor*. New York: Riverhead Books, 1993.

Leong, Kenneth S. *The Zen Teachings of Jesus*. New York: Crossroad, 2001.

Miller, David L. *Christs*. New Orleans: Spring Journal Books, 2005.

Pagels, Elaine. *The Gnostic Gospels*. New York: Vintage Books, 1989.

Smith, Morton. *Jesus the Magician: A Renowned Historian Reveals How Jesus Was Viewed by People of His Time*. San Francisco: Red Wheel/Weiser, 2014.

About the Author

Thomas Moore is the author of the bestselling book *Care of the Soul* and many other books on deepening spirituality and cultivating soul in every aspect of life. He has been a monk, a musician, a university professor, and a psychotherapist, and today he lectures widely on holistic medicine, spirituality, psychotherapy, and the arts. He lectures frequently in Ireland and has a special love of Irish culture.

He has a PhD in religion from Syracuse University and has won several awards for his work, including an honorary doctorate from Lesley University and the Humanitarian Award from Einstein Medical School of Yeshiva University. Three of his books have won the prestigious Books for a Better Life awards. He writes fiction and music and often works with his wife, Hari Kirin, who is an artist and yoga instructor. He writes regular columns for *Spirituality & Health* and the *Huffington Post*. For more about him, visit thomasmooresoul.com.

Thomas Moore is available to speak to your group or at your event. For more information, please contact us at publicity@skylightpaths.com or at (802) 457-4000.

About SKYLIGHT PATHS Publishing

SkyLight Paths Publishing is creating a place where people of different spiritual traditions come together for challenge and inspiration, a place where we can help each other understand the mystery that lies at the heart of our existence.

Through spirituality, our religious beliefs are increasingly becoming a part of our lives—rather than *apart* from our lives. While many of us may be more interested than ever in spiritual growth, we may be less firmly planted in traditional religion. Yet, we do want to deepen our relationship to the sacred, to learn from our own as well as from other faith traditions, and to practice in new ways.

SkyLight Paths sees both believers and seekers as a community that increasingly transcends traditional boundaries of religion and denomination—people wanting to learn from each other, *walking together, finding the way.*

For your information and convenience, at the back of this book we have provided a list of other SkyLight Paths books you might find interesting and useful. They cover the following subjects:

Buddhism / Zen	Gnosticism	Poetry
Catholicism	Hinduism / Vedanta	Prayer
Chaplaincy		Religious Etiquette
Children's Books	Inspiration	Retirement & Later-
Christianity	Islam / Sufism	Life Spirituality
Comparative Religion	Judaism	Spiritual Biography
	Meditation	Spiritual Direction
Earth-Based Spirituality	Mindfulness	Spirituality
	Monasticism	Women's Interest
Enneagram	Mysticism	Worship
Global Spiritual Perspectives	Personal Growth	

Or phone, mail or email to: SKYLIGHT PATHS Publishing
An imprint of Turner Publishing Company
4507 Charlotte Avenue • Suite 100 • Nashville, Tennessee 37209
Tel: (615) 255-2665 • www.skylightpaths.com
Prices subject to change.

For more information about each book, visit our website at www.skylightpaths.com.

9 781683 363453